DEREK

Derek Nimmo has been a household name in Britain for almost twenty years, known and loved by viewers and listeners alike for programmes such as *Just a Nimmo* and *Life Begins at Forty*. He is also well known overseas, especially in Hong Kong, Australia and New Zealand, where he had his own television series and appeared in several successful plays. But his audiences may not realize that he is also a man who loves – and knows – his drink. Here he shares that knowledge with his readers in inimitable Nimmo style, producing the ideal guide for the dedicated drinker who doesn't take his pleasures *too* seriously!

Derek Nimmo's Drinker's Companion

with drawings

by Michael ffolkes

Hamlyn Paperbacks

DEREK NIMMO'S DRINKER'S COMPANION
ISBN 0 600 32152 5

First published in Great Britain 1979
by Hamlyn Paperbacks
Copyright © 1979 by Victorama Ltd

Hamlyn Paperbacks are published by
The Hamlyn Publishing Group Ltd,
Astronaut House,
Feltham,
Middlesex, England

Printed and bound in Great Britain by
Cox & Wyman Ltd, Reading

Acknowledgements

Compiling the chapters on wine for this book would have been impossible without the help of Michael Jacobson, one of the wisest and most entertaining of the world's great authorities on wine. I am most indebted to him, as I am to Arthur Binsted, for teaching me so much about beer, and to Patrick Anthony for introducing me to so many delicious — if near-lethal — cocktails. Finally, I must thank Ann Power for typing out the manuscript so swiftly and accurately — fortified by nothing more than the occasional glass of 'Evelyn's Ambrosia', a unique home-made wine produced in a first floor flat in the sun-kissed Acton region of West London.

Michael Flanders' lyrics on page 77 appear by kind permission of Mrs Claudia Flanders.

Liquid Measures Conversion Table

Table I: Measures and glasses — equivalent capacities

(Table to two points of decimals)

Centilitres (cl)	U.K. fluid ounces (fl oz)	U.S.A. liquid or fluid ounces (lq oz)	Remarks
0.1	0.03	0.03	*Dash = 5 drops*
0.5	0.18	0.17	*Teaspoon = ⅛ fl oz*
			Dessertspoon = ¼ fl oz
1	0.35	0.34	*Tablespoon = ½ fl oz*
2	0.70	0.68	*6-out measure = ⅚ fl oz*
			5-out measure = 1 fl oz
3	1.06	1.01	*4-out measure = 1¼ fl oz*
4	1.40	1.35	*Pony (U.S.A.) = 1 fl oz (approx.)*
5	1.76	1.69	*Jigger (U.S.A.) = 1½ fl oz (approx.)*
6	2.11	2.03	
7	2.46	2.37	*Cocktail glasses vary from 2 to 3½ oz*
8	2.82	2.71	*2½ oz is an average U.K. size*
9	3.17	3.04	
10	3.52	3.38	
11	3.87	3.72	
12	4.22	4.06	*4-oz wine glass (U.S.A.); a*
13	4.58	4.40	*good size for Sours, like vodka and tomato juice*

(Table to two points of decimals)

Centilitres (cl)	U.K. fluid ounces (fl oz)	U.S.A. liquid or fluid ounces (lq oz)	Remarks
14	4.93	4.73	*A U.K. size is a 5-oz wine glass*
15	5.28	5.07	*14.2 cl = 5 fl oz = 1 Gill or Noggin*
16	5.63	5.41	
17	5.98	5.75	
18	6.34	6.09	
19	6.69	6.42	
20	7.04	6.77	
21	7.39	7.10	
22	7.74	7.44	
23	8.10	7.78	*23 cl = U.K. 8-oz wine glass*
24	8.45	8.12	
25	8.80	8.45	
26	9.15	8.80	
27	9.50	9.13	
28	9.85	9.47	*28.4 cl = 10 fl oz = U.K. half-pint*
29	10.21	9.81	*Tumblers can be smaller, but 10 oz gives wider scope*
30	10.56	10.14	*33 cl = 12-oz wine glass*
50	17.60	16.91	*56 cl = U.K. pint*
75	26.40	25.36	*75 cl = One 'Reputed' Quart = usual wine bottle*
100	35.20	33.81	*100 cl = 1 litre*

1.14 litres = 40 fl oz = 8.0 gills = One Imperial Quart = ¼ Imperial Gallon.

Contents

Introduction

My father drove me to drink.

I don't mean that literally, of course, but he was a teetotaller and I, like so many people, have spent most of my life trying to do the things that my father didn't.

My father didn't drink, but my grandmother did – though not in the way my statement might imply! She just enjoyed the occasional glass of sherry and it was she who introduced me to the charms of alcohol. When I was quite small, she took me to a pub in Nottingham called The Trip to Jerusalem. It was an unusual pub because it had historical associations – the Crusaders had paused there for light refreshements on their way to the wars – so that children under age were allowed to visit the pub for historical rather than alcoholic reasons. My grandmother was interested in history as well as alcohol and wanted me to share her enthusiasms. She was a delightful woman. Canny too. She always gave me a peppermint before taking me home.

Nowadays, I don't drink much sherry, but I do drink quite a lot of wine. The reason I have devoted so much of this book to wine is that it's my favourite form of liquid refreshment. When I'm working in the theatre, I don't drink anything all day, but I do look forward to a delicious bottle of wine when I get home at night. I'd be happy to share it with my wife, but she prefers Perrier water. For her, drinking is a spectator sport.

One of the great advantages of working on this *Drinker's Companion* is that it has given me a legitimate excuse to raid my own cellar. I'm down to my last three bottles of Château d'Yquem 1945 and I've just discovered that these days they're fetching around £200 a bottle! Now I've got to find friends of sufficient calibre to share the final three bottles with me. I romped through the other twenty-one without a care, but now that I know how much each sip is worth I don't dare touch the stuff. I've got a bottle of 1840 claret that David Frost once gave me and I don't dare touch that either!

My favourite white wines come from the Loire. I've explored its whole length, from Muscadet right up to Sancerre, and it is a pilgrimage well worth making. Some of my favourite red wines come from Australia. I have four bottles of the magnificent 1961 Grange Hermitage, one of the finest wines ever to emerge from Australia. I should have rather more of it than I do because I was given a dozen bottles when I was in Australia recently. The bottles, in a case, travelled with me from Adelaide to Melbourne, from Melbourne to Hobart, from Hobart to Launceston, from Launceston to Canberra, from Canberra to Singapore, from Singapore to Dubai, and no harm came to them. But when they reached that ridiculous revolving suitcase crusher at Heathrow, their fate was sealed. I was only able to rescue four unbroken bottles from a great pool of vintage Grange Hermitage!

There is a lot in the book about wines and cocktails because I love them. There is not so much about beer, because I'm no great authority on the subject and I only really drink beer when I've been out tramping in the country. When you've been ploughing through meadows, and along muddy bridle paths in gumboots, there is nothing nicer than to end the expedition with bread and cheese and a pint of bitter.

I must make it clear that I do also drink non-alcoholic liquids — even water, especially the world's finest, which you can find at a beautiful mineral spring north of Melbourne called Hepburn's Spa. I do most of my real drinking at home over a meal, but as well as Hepburn's Spa, I have a number of other favourite – if somewhat more intoxicating – 'watering holes' in different parts of the world.

In London, I love Jules Bar in Jermyn Street. It is permanently old-fashioned, has very good and imaginative cocktails, and a live pianist, so one gets the feeling of faded splendour, which is rather reassuring.

In the rest of Britain, I like the country pubs. I'm very fond of The Sign of the Angel at Laycock where the food is as fine as the wine. Abroad, of course, I love the very grand hotels, like the Oriental in Bangkok – which has a fine cellar and an excellent bar – and the Mount Nelson in Cape Town. Because I'm generally looking for good food as well as drink, there is one restaurant in Bangkok that I go to whenever I am there. It is more like a zoo than a restaurant: they have things on the menu like tiger salad and bear steaks, and you have to order the elephant knuckle twenty-four hours in advance so that they can defrost it. Most of the things on the menu I've never ordered. There is also something called a Bat Cocktail and to order it is macabre and disgusting because they have the bats all hanging upside down at the back of the restaurant *live* and, rather like choosing a trout, you choose your bat and they spead it out by its wings and slit its throat, catching the blood in a glass for you to drink! If you have too many, you end up looking like Christopher Lee.

Of all life's pleasures I put drinking very high. It would be insulting to my beautiful wife to say that I value wine above sex, but I am *very* fond of wine. I put wine so high on my list of pleasures because if you drink sufficient of it nothing else matters!

I always feel I'm much less boring when I have had a glass of wine – which is my excuse for having one with every chapter in the book. Why don't you join me? Take my word for it, if you read my *Drinker's Companion* with a glass in your hand you'll find it twice as entertaining.

15

After all, to read a book about drink without one is nothing less than *sacrilege*.

Cheers!

Wine — What Is It?

The French have a saying: 'A day without wine is a day without sun.' Perhaps not very apt for our particular climate, yet the basic point is true enough. Wine is part of the good life — and not restricted to a wealthy few but increasingly open to all of us. It improves a meal; it comforts the tummy and eases tensions; it creates a friendly atmosphere and encourages good conversation. Taken in moderation, as it always should be, it is directly beneficial to the health. But above all, wine is there to be enjoyed.

Wine is a natural, living substance. According to a formal dictionary definition, it is the naturally fermented juice of freshly gathered grapes, made in the district where those grapes were grown. But that gives no inkling of what makes the juice so special: of the vast range of different wines and the endless fascination afforded by their innumerable variations in taste, scent and colour. Nor can a formal definition convey anything of the scrupulous care required to turn the juice into wine that is palatable and appealing. The wine grower faces an infinity of patient tasks each year — hoeing, weeding, pruning, tidying, spraying, grafting, then harvesting the grapes, pressing them, fermenting the juice (called the 'must') and maturing the resultant wine in casks, perhaps for several years before it is bottled.

The French also have a favourite story about a gay old Parisian connoisseur who boasted that water had never touched his lips. Asked what he used for brushing his

'Ah, you look like a man who knows something about wine.'

teeth in, he replied: 'A glass of light Sauternes, my boy!'

While you may not feel inclined to go to quite such lengths, it is a fact that you can find wines which are suitable for virtually any occasion, and not just with meals. For instance, to give you a fillip in a dreary mid-morning, as a cool refresher on a hot summer's afternoon, and, of course, as a pretty inexpensive way of throwing a party at any time of the day or night.

A TWELVE-MONTH JOB

On the subject of what has to be done to transform the grape juice into wine, it's not for me to question the accuracy of the Good Book, but I do feel that its treatment of that business about Naboth's vineyard must raise suspicions that somebody withheld at least one part of the truth. If only Jezebel had been warned of the sweat involved in tending the property, she would surely have refrained from going to such lengths to filch it for her spouse. But then, of course, there'd have been no story.

In another particular, though, the Biblical scribes were right on the button. When Naboth refused to sell his inherited vineyard to King Ahab — doubtless at a good price, too — he was all too typical of those obstinate men of the soil who don't know what's good for them. How else to explain their dogged preference for a back-breaking existence instead of some far easier way of making a living? For if you should ever be in a position to run a vineyard, you'll find that, unlike almost any other form of agriculture, your one crop will require continual, non-stop devotion. Throughout the twelve months of the year, it doesn't allow you a single breathing-space.

It may be that you come from a family which has tended the vine for centuries, that you have grown up imbued with traditions of scrupulous care and endless patience and with an instinctive love of the earth and of all the sights and smells with which God has blessed it. In which case, naturally, no other way of life is conceivable, happily for all of us!

So far as the vineyard year has a beginning and end, which it really doesn't, I suppose it could be said to start in the autumn, immediately after the harvest. The actual period when the grapes are picked varies considerably, depending on differences in climate, soil, the nature of the wine grown and a whole host of other factors. It is late September or October in most of the leading French vineyards, but elsewhere in Europe it can be as early as August or as late as November.

For similar reasons, each wine farmer has his own methods, liable to differ in some slight degree of practice or timing from those of his neighbours. The following account, therefore, is only a broad outline and may well have variations in detail from region to region.

To get some idea of the complexities, one need merely start by looking at the range of soils involved. Some of Europe's best white wines, for instance, are produced in soil with a predominance of chalk and limestone. The Champagne district, the Loire valley, the best German and Alsace vineyards, and the white areas of Bordeaux and Burgundy, are all calcareous in character. The delicate Moselles are grown on steep hillsides composed almost entirely of slate. On the other hand, Médoc's fine red wines are grown in gravel overlying sand and clay; the best sherries come from grapes grown in the lightest soil of the Jerez region; in the Douro region, where port is made, the vines often have to be planted by blasting holes into the barren, schistous slopes of the steep mountainsides; and in the southern part of the Rhône valley, vineyards will not be recognized for quality wines unless their surface is covered with a mass of hefty boulders.

Generally speaking, clay in the soil helps to produce red wines with a higher alcoholic content and deeper colour (as in Burgundy and the St Emilion district). But too

20

much clay can result in rich yet flabby wines, without much distinction in bouquet or flavour. It is generally true that the best wines are made from grapes grown on unpromising soil which is little or no use for any other crop. The harder a vine has to fight for survival, it seems, the better the qualities it achieves.

Now take into account the varying effects of weather on the many different types of grape. For example, one of the best-known grapes in the Bordeaux region, the Cabernet Sauvignon, scores over other types by being exceptionally resistant to harmful decay from undue damp; against this, it has to be specially protected from a fungus called oidium, to which it is more susceptible than many other grapes.

Another well-known grape, the Merlot, is highly resistant to oidium but is vulnerable to mildew. Yet another type, the Malbec, is useful because it matures quickly but has the snag of being liable to drop its fruit at an early stage.

Still with me? That fine wines continue to be produced in huge quantities, despite all the problems which may arise, seems little short of a miracle. That the miracle does happen, year in, year out, is convincing proof of the patient skill and pride in craftmanship of the individual wine-grower.

His first job, after the year's crop of grapes has been picked, is to carry out extensive hoeing of the vineyard – usually in October – followed by banking up of the earth round each vine stem, to protect the plant from frost during the winter months. From November to March, the vines must also be pruned — enough to prevent over-production and maintain their quality, but not so much as to impair their vigour. Many vineyard workers have such skill at the job that they know exactly how many bunches of grapes each single plant produced in previous years and can gauge the extent of pruning it requires accordingly. Throughout this period, hoeing and ploughing continue until the time comes to train the grape-bearing branches along string or wire. In most French and German vineyards, the vines are planted in orderly rows, about a metre (3–4 ft) apart, and the lowest bunches of grapes will be kept 45–60cm (1½–2 ft) above the ground, so that they can benefit from the warmth of the earth while ripening. But elsewhere the vine may be trained upwards like a tall bush, while in some parts of Italy, Spain and Portugal, and in Madeira above all, it is trained along overhead wires or trellises anything up to 3.5 metres (12 ft) in height — mainly because the earth becomes just too hot for the grapes in the summer months.

In March, too, a special plough is used in some areas to uncover the vine stems. Then, in April, they are covered again and furrows are left to allow the spring rains to escape. Once the rainwater has gone, the special plough comes into action once more and uncovers the roots ready for fruiting.

The spring is also the time for replanting those parts of the vineyard where unproductive old vines have been uprooted. Most new vines take seven years to produce wine ot good quality and thereafter they have an economic life of anything from twenty to fifty years. So winegrowers usually try to maintain stretches of vines in ascending age groups, to ensure the consistency of overall quality as well as avoiding sporadic drops in the volume of production – bearing in mind that once old vines have been pulled up the soil in which they were planted is allowed to remain fallow for several years. (In the Côtes du Rhône, indeed, it may be up to twenty years.)

Another major task is to graft the young vines on to American shoots. This is necessary because of a tiny beetle-like pest, the phylloxera, which came near to destroying Europe's vineyards in the latter half of the nineteenth century. It was found that unlike the European vine stock (*Vitis vinifera*), used in almost all the world's principal wine-growing regions, the native American wild vines were resistant to phylloxera. Grafting Europe's vines on to these resistant stocks was the only solution, and the disease is so virulent that the practice has to be continued to this day in all but a handful of vineyards.

The blossom usually appears in mid-June, and a fresh round of pruning begins in order to strengthen the eventual fruit – lightly for some grape varieties, severely for others. Subsequently, once the grape berries have formed properly, the soil is ploughed yet again to cover the foot of the vines.

Now the pattern of pruning will be reversed, with heavier cutting back for the vines treated lightly before, and vice-versa. During the spring and early summer months, too, various sprays are applied to protect the plants: for example, copper sulphate to counteract mildew, and dry sulphur (about 18 kilos per hectare, or 16 lb per acre) against oidium.

But all spraying has to stop a few weeks before the harvest, when a fine grey dust begins to appear on the grape skins – the natural yeasts essential to the winemaking process. By this time, the grapes will have reached their full size, and from about the first week of August they start to ripen, their colour gradually turning darker.

From then on, the farmer can only pray for hot, but not excessive, sun by day and no more than a modicum of moisture or rain showers at night. If there are heavy rainfalls, with the attendant risk of mildew, there is virtually nothing he can do about it. The sole answer in that case, reducing his total yield, is to have the affected grapes cut away from the rest when vintage time arrives.

It is small wonder that the conclusion of a successful vintage is always marked by a generous beanfeast for the vineyard workers – just for a night or two, before getting on with the job once more. In face of all the arduous difficulties to be overcome in bringing us the pleasures of

23

good wine, the rest of us just have to be grateful that there are still so many Naboths around.

THE ORIGINS OF WINE

In addition to the countries I have already mentioned, others where wines are produced in fair to large quantities include Spain (third behind France and Italy), Algeria, Australia, Austria, Bulgaria, Canada, Cyprus, Czechoslovakia, Egypt, England (quite a dramatic revival in recent years), Greece, Hungary, Israel, Luxembourg, Malta, Mexico, New Zealand, Portugal, South Africa, Switzerland, Turkey, the United States and the U.S.S.R. From that spread, it can readily be deduced that winemaking has been with the world for rather a long time. As witness Genesis IX, verses 20–21:

> 'And Noah began to be an husbandman, and he planted a vineyard; and he drank of the wine, and was drunken; and he was uncovered within his tent.'

– a passage which gives some credence to the belief that the production of wine is older than recorded history!

In fact, fossils of ancient vines have been discovered (*Vitis germanica* and *Vitis icelandica*) which date back to the Tertiary period some million or more years ago. However, they differed completely from the *Vitis vinifera*, the vine known today as the 'European vine' and now used in nearly all the principal wine-growing areas of the world.

Vines will grow in any temperate climate and require only a period of winter rest and no tremendous extremes of heat and cold – perhaps just the conditions found after the glacial ages. Accordingly, it is reasonable to suppose that, when Neanderthal man buried his dead with food and hunting implements about 50,000 years ago, he may

24

already have known the joys of the juice of fully-ripened grapes. Certainly, when the fourth glacial age softened towards more temperate conditions and man followed the food and plants to which he was accustomed, grapes would have been amongst the foods he found. So, when Neolithic man settled in the 'fertile crescent' – the area bending north from Egypt through Palestine and Syria, and turning south again through the valleys of the Tigris and Euphrates – all the materials were available for him to produce wine.

Since the vine is pictured on tablets carved during the earliest dynasties in Egypt one can perhaps date the wine trade proper as being some 10,000 years old. By the time of Rameses III, in the twentieth dynasty, the 40-metre (133 ft) long Papyrus Harris recorded 513 vineyards amongst the property of the temples. Excavations in Egypt have produced evidence of wine production which has continued unbroken up to the present day. The ancient Greeks, too, had a great knowledge of wine, as illustrated by the discovery of a jar stopper, in Mersin, dating back to 4000 B.C. In those days, man was largely concentrated in the Eastern Mediterranean. But by 700 B.C. Phoenician and Carthaginian traders were seeking fresh fields – and the Phoenicians, landing near Marseilles to travel overland to collect tin from Cornwall, established vineyards at staging posts on the way. The most famous of these, perhaps, is the Côte-Rôtie, just south of Lyons.

Most present-day European vineyards were founded during the growth of the Roman Empire. In the first and second centuries B.C., the Romans had travelled as far north as the Baltic and westwards across Europe, establishing the classical vineyards we now know as Bordeaux, Burgundy, Champagne, the Rhine and the Moselle. With the fall of the Roman Empire came the end of the first era of vintage wines. Subsequently, the people of Burgundy got into the charming habit – particularly when they had been naughty – of making gifts of vineyards to the monasteries. (One of these is now the world-famous Clos de Vougeot.)

In Germany, never a country to do things by halves, a similar practice led the clerics to own more land, for several centuries, than anyone else in the realm.

In medieval England, there were between 100 and 150 vineyards, apparently scattered across twenty-four counties — from Worcestershire, with seventeen, and Essex, with sixteen, down to Buckinghamshire, Devon, Hampshire and Norfolk, which probably had one each. The Domesday Book, in the late eleventh century, records thirty-five vineyards covering a total of 123 acres (50 hectares) — about 3½ acres (1.5 hectares) apiece. It has taken the English close on eight centuries to get back to that happy state of affairs. But the industry, albeit still small-scale compared with the Continental giants, is now expanding quite rapidly each year and producing light white wines of a quality fully matching many better-known European equivalents. Suffice it to say that you'll find some these days on such august wine lists as that of the Q.E. II.

Apart from gifts to the Church and the early monks' need, quite often, to grow their own wine for mass, adventure and exploration have also been responsible for many wines. During the Crusades, the Knights Templar grew well accustomed to wine. So, when forced to leave the Holy Land, they established vineyards in their succeeding homes — notably Cyprus, where their castle at Kolossi, in the centre of their main command district, the Grande Commanderia, gave its name to at least one brand of wine, Commanderia, which remains very popular to this day. This, indeed, is probably the oldest *continuous* wine, as it were, in the world. It's the self-same 'Cypriot Noma' lauded by the poets and historians of Ancient Greece and Rome.

The youngest major wine-growing area is Australia, where vineyards were established within three years of the

Union Jack first being flown over Port Jackson, near Sydney, in 1788. In 1801, an expert sent by Napoleon forecast that Australia would become the 'Vineyard of Great Britain'. That hasn't actually happened, but the country does now have a wine industry with a total capital investment of well over £100 million!

The prediction by Napoleon's expert probably reflected (unfounded) French fears that, once peace returned, the English might be lost as the principal export market for Bordeaux. They had been so for some 600 years — though originally the wine was seldom like the wine we know today. The ancients knew very little about fermentation and preserved their wine by the addition of honey, spices and sometimes herbs. The big breakthrough on that score did not come until 1866, when Louis Pasteur revealed the previously unknown principles of fermentation, enabling growers to exercise complete control of the process and to produce wines, even in ordinary years, with a much higher alcoholic content than had normally been possible before. Nowadays, the wine industry uses modern machinery, advanced techniques of soil analysis, the knowledge of taste origins derived from liquid gas chromotography, and many other scientific aids. Each has merely reinforced the words of Benjamin Franklin: 'Wine is a constant proof that God loves us and wants to see us happy.'

THE MAIN TYPES

Despite the wide range of producing countries and the enormous choice in the shops, there are really only five broad categories of wine: white, red and rosé (pink), sparkling, and stronger, fortified wines (e.g. port and sherry).

Still, light wines — those from the EEC countries being familiarly known as 'table wines' — are always white, red

'Forget about the colour and the bouquet. Just ask yourself, does it blow your mind?'

or rosé, though the actual shade of their colour can vary enormously.

White wines range from very pale straw or slightly greenish tints up to a deep yellow or gold. In general, the lighter the shade, the drier the wine; and the yellower it is, the sweeter it will be. But that is not an invariable rule; to make sure, check with your wine merchant.

Red wines range from deep purple through ruby to very pale, transparent shades. Rosé wines, too, may have anything from the faintest tinge of pink up to a deep pink that is only just short of red.

The leading wine-growing countries, such as France, Italy and Spain, make *all* types of wine — the main exception being Germany, where white wines (hocks and Moselles) account for 98 % of total production. The range and variety of wines in existence is so vast that it would be quite impossible to list them all. As a very rough guide, though, here are just a few of the principal European types you are likely to find in the majority of local wine shops:

White

Dry and light-bodied

Austria:	Dry, white
California:	Pinot Chardonnay
England:	Dry, white
France:	Entre-deux-Mers, Graves, Muscadet, Pouilly Fumé, Chablis, Alsace Sylvaner
Germany:	Steinwein, Kasel
Hungary:	Balatoni Furmint
Italy:	Orvieto Secco, Soave, Verdicchio
Portugal:	Vinho Verde
Spain:	From Catalonia region
Yugoslavia:	Lutomer Laski Riesling

Dry and full-bodied

France:	Mâcon Blanc, Pouilly Fuissé, Alsace Riesling, Gewurztraminer, Meursault, Puligny-Montrachet
Germany:	Rudesheimer, Johannisberger
Hungary:	Balatoni Riesling
Italy:	Frascati Secco
South Africa:	Paarl
Spain:	Rioja, Valdepenas
Yugoslavia:	Lutomer Sylvaner

Medium-dry to medium-sweet

Australia:	Barossa Riesling
Austria:	Gumpoldskirchner
France:	Entre-deux-Mers, Graves Supérieures, Vouvray
Germany:	Niersteiner, Oppenheimer, Piesporter
Italy:	Frascati Abboccato, Orvieto Abboccato
South Africa:	Steen
Spain:	Rioja, and from La Mancha region

Sweet

France:	Sauternes, Barsac, Monbazillac
Germany:	(Vineyard) Auslese, (Vineyard) Beerenauslese
Hungary:	Tokay Aszu
Italy:	Moscato
Spain:	Valencia, Malaga
Yugoslavia:	Tiger Milk

Red

Dry and light-bodied

France:	Lighter clarets such as Bordeaux Rouge, Médoc; southern Burgundies

	(e.g. Beaujolais, Fleurie, Mâcon); Midi wines such as Corbières, Roussillon
Italy:	Barbera, Bardolino, Valpolicella
Spain:	From Catalonia region

Dry and full-bodied

Australia:	Tahbilk Estate Cabernet
California:	Cabernet Sauvignon
France:	Fuller clarets such as St Emilion, Pomerol; Côte d'Or Burgundies; Côtes du Rhône; Côtes de Provence
Hungary:	Egri Bikaver (Bull's Blood)
Israel:	Carmel Avdat
Italy:	Chianti, Barolo
Portugal:	Dâo
South Africa:	Roodeberg
Spain:	Rioja, and from La Mancha region
Yugoslavia:	Burgundec

Sweet

(Sweet red table wines are very unusual, but there are exceptions)

Cyprus:	Commandaria
Italy:	Lambrusco
Portugal:	Lisbon
Spain:	From Tarragona and Valencia regions

Rosé

Dry and medium-dry

France:	Provence, Anjou, Tavel
Israel:	Palwin Rosé

Italy:	From Lake Garda region
Portugal:	Various slightly sparkling rosé wines
Spain:	Alicante and from Catalonia region

This brief selection, of course, does not include the various ranges of inexpensive branded table wines, which have been blended to meet what market research has established as prevailing public tastes and which are often very good value for everyday drinking purposes. Nor can the wines I have listed give anything more than a faint inkling of just how many there are to choose from. Let us have a closer look, now, at some of the best known.

Claret

The French habitually class Bordeaux as the queen of wines — which, in accordance with the traditional Gallic attitude to women, implies that they are lighter, subtler and just that much greater than the wines of their royal consort, Burgundy. Extending the metaphor, they often wear better and live longer, too. . . . So it is perhaps ironic that, for all the French gallantry, the first people to put Bordeaux wines in the number one position were those stolid, passionless unimaginative folk — the English!

The local Gascons originally called their wines 'clairet' or 'clairette', meaning that they were lighter and clearer than all others of the time. The English, or course, immediately mispronounced the name . . . and it is by their word, claret, that the red wines of Bordeaux have been generally known to the world ever since.

Another familiar term springs from the medieval English merchants who sent their vessels to Bordeaux to buy and ship back the local wines. Hence the word 'shippers', still applied to firms dealing in the wine export trade, even though they no longer own the actual vessels involved.

In the Bordeaux region itself, the English association

remains enshrined in several of the localities . . . hardly surprising, since the area did in fact belong to perfidious Albion for some 300 years, throughout the reigns of ten English kings. Just to show what's what, the region still boasts a Château Smith and a Château Brown!

Château Talbot, in the St Julien district, was named after John Talbot, first Earl of Shrewsbury, the commander who finally lost Bordeaux to the French at the Battle of Castillon in 1453. The town of Libourne, east of Bordeaux, was named after Roger de Leybourne, a top functionary of England's King Henry III. There is even a legend that Château Haut-Brion, home of one of the five greatest 'growths', was a local corruption of the Irish name O'Brien — presumably the French getting their own back for what the English did to *their* language!

Bordeaux has dealt in wine for more than 2000 years, though the commercial development of its own vineyards was interrupted in A.D. 92 by the decree of the Roman Emperor Domitian, who tried to give Italian wines a monopoly by ordering all other vineyards throughout the Empire to be uprooted — a decree finally rescinded by the Emperor Probus in the year 270. Even so, early Roman records at Bordeaux mention the presence of a 'negotiator Britannicus' — an English dealer who could surely have been there only for the purpose of buying wine.

However, England's close relations with the region date back officially to the arranged marriage in May, 1152, between nineteen-year-old Henry Plantagenet (later Henry II) and Eleanor of Aquitaine, then aged about thirty. The dowry Eleanor brought with her included much of western France, of which the wine-growing areas formed the richest jewel.

Oddly enough, though, it was 'bad' King John who really got things going. His mother lived in a château near Bordeaux and, at the beginning of his reign in 1199, he encouraged the firm establishment of the wine trade with England by exempting the local growers from export taxes. John also made free grants of land near Bordeaux, on condition it was put into good order and planted with vineyards — a practice continued by Henry III and Edward I. So it is fair to say that the original foundation of a good number of Bordeaux's finest growths was inspired by English royalty. Just how close the links were is shown by the fact that Henry de Galeys, Mayor of London in 1274, was Mayor of Bordeaux the following year.

Today, the Bordeaux region covers slightly under 13,000 square kilometres (5000 square miles), of which about one tenth are under vine. The vineyards are divided among something like 60,000 proprietors, with about 2000 making the greatest wines. Altogether, they produce upwards of 400 million litres (90 million gallons) of red, white and rosé wine each year.

But their fame rests on quality, not quantity. Bordeaux is responsible for nearly one-third of all the top-grade wines in France.

Back in 1855, an official committee classified the sixty-two best clarets into five 'crus', or growths. The 'Premiers Crus', top of the tree, were restricted to four chateaux: Lafite, Margaux, Latour and Haut-Brion, (to which Château Mouton-Rothschild was added only a few years ago).

Fifteen growths were classed as 'Deuxièmes Crus' (including such celebrated names as Châteaux Gruaud-Larose, Leoville-Lascases and Montrose).

The 'Troisièmes Crus' comprised fourteen growths, those particularly familiar abroad including Château Kirwan, Château Palmer and Château Calon-Segur. Eleven more became 'Quatrièmes Crus' (e.g. Château Talbot and Château Beychevelle), and finally eighteen were classed as 'Cinquièmes Crus'.

The committee based its reasoning on the average price levels of these world-famous wines over much of the preceding century, deeming it safe to assume that the higher the price merchants were prepared to pay, the better the wine. Although, with the passage of time, changes up and down have naturally intervened, the initial grading of the top wines still broadly holds good. However, one of the great joys of Bordeaux is that, with such a multiplicity of growers, there are hundreds more wines which are almost as good — and maybe of equal stature, in top years. Below the 'Grands Crus' are other classifications — 'Bourgeois', 'artisan' or peasant growths — which can sometimes be of extremely high quality.

Most of the small producers now sell their wine to co-operatives or, through brokers, to the big shipping houses, who will often blend them with others to make up a standard wine. To this day, however, when visiting the region, you may still come across tiny individual vineyards producing wine in limited quantity which is a treasure in its own right.

Two main factors account for the consistently high quality associated with claret. First, geography. Most of the vineyards lie along or fairly near the banks of three great rivers — the Garonne and the Dordogne, which join 24 kilometres (15 miles) above Bordeaux to form the mighty Gironde, flowing northwards into the Bay of Biscay. The proximity of the sea ensures a damp atmosphere, valuable for swelling the grapes before harvest. At the same time, the sea breezes have a moderating influence on the climate, preventing too great a difference between summer and winter temperatures. Much of the soil is generally characterized by gravel or pebbles. These store up the heat of the sun during the day, giving it back to the grapes at night, which, again, helps to reduce extremes of temperature and also ensures that the lower bunches of grapes ripen well.

The second key factor is the natural purity of the wine. In general, its production follows the method established since Roman times: the long round of care up to the harvest in late September, the pressing, fermentation, racking and eventual bottling or despatch in casks. There may be some variations — for instance, removal or reduction of the grape-stalks before pressing, to lessen the amount of tannin and thus permit the wine to mature more quickly. But the all-important difference from other wines is that in Bordeaux it is forbidden to add extra alcohol to the wine. Because of this, claret has the 'gift of age', maturing slowly in cask until old enough to be bottled, then growing to perfection in bottle and remaining at its peak for many years. A great claret might well live on for a century or more.

Burgundy

Legend has it that, towards the end of the eighteenth century, a Napoleonic officer called Colonel Bisson, marching northwards to join the army on the Rhine, halted his troops outside the gates of an old Cistercian monastery a few miles south of Dijon and ordered them to 'present arms'. The colonel was saluting not the monks but a wine which took its name from the monastery — Clos de Vougeot, one of the great wines of Burgundy. In that revolutionary period, the colonel seemed to be making the point that, whatever France's troubles, here at least was a symbol of continuity, a supreme French achievement that would never die.

Alas! Latter-day historians assert that the story is quite apocryphal. Even if it didn't happen, though, the legend has has such appeal that it has often taken hold in practice. Many French troops (or Air Force planes) *do* give the monastery a salute when they happen to pass by. Doubtless they share the feelings of lovers of historical romance in other countries, to whom the very name Burgundy conjures up visions of gallantry and regal splendour. Dashing swordsmen, whose skill was matched only by their love of the good things of life ... the dukes of Burgundy, sporting cloaks of deep wine-red hue, whose power was shown in early plays as equal if not superior to that of the kings of France.

As we saw with claret, the French themselves maintain the royal theme in describing Burgundy as the king of wines, to Bordeaux's queen.

Within the Burgundy region, in turn, its most famous wines are often classed similarly in regal terms: Chambertin as the king, Romanée-Conti as the queen, Close de Vougeot as the regent, and about seven more wines are accorded the status of 'members of the royal family'.

Despite these monarchical trappings and the age-old renown of Burgundy wines, the vineyards cover a much smaller area, relatively, than most people realize. Following a shoulder-shaped line from Chablis south-easterly to Dijon and then south-south-west in the direction of Lyons, the vineyards extend in a strip of about 280 kilometres (175 miles), with a couple of sizeable gaps. But along several stretches, the strip is under a kilometre in width. Altogether, about 50,000 hectares (125,000 acres) are under vine, compared with some 130,000 hectares (320,000 acres) in the Bordeaux region.

On top of this, most of the individual vineyards are a good deal smaller and each is also divided among a number of different owners. For example, Clos de Vougeot, easily the biggest Burgundy vineyard, covers 50 hectares (125 acres) — split among about fifty owners.

Contrast this with Bordeaux, where the celebrated claret, Château Margaux, has some 97 hectares (240 acres) in single ownership and even the most difficult claret for ordinary folk to come by, Château Lafite, traditionally the greatest of Bordeaux wines, has 60 hectares (150 acres) under vine.

Against these, the vineyards of Burgundy's 'king', Chambertin, and the adjoining Clos de Bèze cover only 28 hectacres (70 acres), while the 'queen', Romanée-Conti, has a less than 2 hectares (a mere 4½ acres). Little wonder that their wines command prices in keeping with their regal exclusiveness!

In general, the wines of Burgundy are distinguished for their fullness and robust characters and their rich bouquets. But it is a misconception to regard them as always 'heavier' than clarets. To quote the great André Simon: 'The difference between them is not one of "quality" but of "tone", just as the voice of a soprano differs from that of a contralto not necessarily in quality but inevitably in tone. We may prefer one to the other or we may, and I certainly do, love them both equally.'

Another frequent misconception is to think of Burgundy solely for its red wines. The finest white wines of Burgundy, such as Montrachet and Corton Charlemagne, out-rank all others in France except the classic Sauternes. The clue to Burgundy's greatness lies in its soil — clay, limestone, silicate and gravel, with a prominent trace of iron. This is ideal for the Pinot grapes, cultivated on the slopes of the region's shallow hills and producing its top quality wines. Another grape variety, the Gamay, is often planted on the upper slopes and the plains; it is hardier than the Pinot, with a bigger yield, producing less expensive wines which can sometimes be drunk very young.

The region starts in the north with Chablis, synonymous for its clean, dry white wines — pale yellow, almost greenish in colour. Some Frenchmen tend to class Chablis separately, but it *is* a true white Burgundy, although there is a jump of nearly 64 kilometres (40 miles) to Dijon. Similarly, the often-separated Beaujolais region, in the south, also comes within the official map of Burgundy wines.

What most people understand by Burgundy, at its pinnacle, starts just south of Dijon, in the Côte d'Or (the golden slope). It is sub-divided into the Côte de Nuits and the Côte de Beaune. From this strip, barely 45 kilometres (27 miles) in length overall, come such hallowed growths as

Chambertin, Clos de Bèze, Clos de Tart, Musigny, Les Bonnes Mares, Clos de Vougeot, Les Grands Echézaux, Romanée, Richebourg, La Tache and Nuits St Georges.

Those are the principal 'greats' from the 20 kilometres (12 miles) of the Côte de Nuits alone. In the 25 kilometres (15 miles) of the Côte de Beaune, immediately to the south, lie other household names like Aloxe-Corton, Clos du Rui, Pommard, Volnay, Meursault, Montrachet and Santenay.

The town of Beaune itself, still with its medieval ramparts, is dominated by a hospital and home for the aged poor, the Hospices de Beaune, founded in 1443 by Nicolas Rolin, Chancellor of the Duchy of Burgundy. He and his wife each endowed it with some of their vineyards, and over the centuries their example was followed by other pious owners. In consequence, the Hospices now own some 65 hectares (160 acres), of which thirty produce top-quality wines, both red and white. These are sold by public auction in the Market Hall of Beaune on the third Sunday in November each year, the wines subsequently bearing a special label with the words 'Hospices de Beaune' followed by the specific vineyard. The annual auctions are always surrounded by delightful festivities, with banquets and wine tastings throughout the weekend. Yet it is far from being just a social occasion. The sales still provide the funds for running the old people's hospital. In addition, while the auction prices may sometimes be a little exaggerated, they provide a yardstick by which the prices of other Burgundies may be assessed.

At the southernmost end of the Burgundy strip, one enters the broader stretches of Mâcon (better known for its white wines) and the ever-popular Beaujolais, where red wines make up 99% of production. These light, fragrant, refreshing young wines offer an abundance of treasures in the Burgundy style, but at considerably lower prices than many of the big-name growths of Côte d'Or. Many wine drinkers abroad are already fond of the most distinguished growths from this region, without always realizing that they are, in fact, Beaujolais — familiar names like Morgan, Moulin-a-Vent, St Amour, Fleurie, Julienas, Chiroubles and Brouilly. Two of the special joys of Beaujolais are that it can often be quaffed as a long drink (cool, from a silver tankard, is one hedonistic delight!) and that it can be produced so as to be drunk at a very early stage. Races to get the year's first supplies in mid-November have become quite a craze in recent times, the acquisition of these consignments being something of a status symbol.

On a loftier plain, a word of caution is necessary about some of those rich-sounding, long-drawn out Burgundy names you often find on restaurant wine lists. They are not necessarily the best. One of the Burgundy region's traditions is that neighbours of a great vineyard may attach their village name to it, for their own wines. These may well be very good, and usually are, but they will not be as supreme as the master whose name forms part of their title.

A prime example is the celebrated Gevrey-Chambertin — a fine wine in its own right, yet never in the class of Chambertin, *tout court*. So, with one or two exceptions, it is a good rule-of-thumb that the shorter the name, the greater the Burgundy. The basic point underlying all this is that unlike the château-bottling of Bordeaux, relatively little Burgundy is bottled for export by its growers. Château-bottled clarets carry their own implicit guarantee, but with Burgundy, most of the bottling is carried out by the shippers, who buy the wine in bulk. A good number of these shipping firms have been in the business for 200 years or more, and their name on the bottle is an equal guarantee.

To make sure that you get what you pay for, therefore, you should always buy your Burgundies through wine merchants and shippers who have earned reputations, over the years, which are every bit as honourable as those of the wares they sell.

Hock

As with claret, the word 'hock' is an entirely English invention, unrecognized in its own country. It was derived from the town of Hochheim and was first used by English gentry in the seveteenth century to describe any light white wine from Germany. At that time, Hochheim was the principal river port from which Rhine wine was shipped.

I wonder what name they would have found for the wine in A.D. 800 if they'd known about it then? For it is, in fact, getting on for 1200 years since the mighty Emperor Charlemagne looked out of his new castle at Ingelheim one cold day early in March and made a discovery for which we can all be grateful. He noticed that, although most of the surrounding valley slopes were still clad in white, the winter snow had already begun to melt on the hills of Johannisberg, on the opposite side of the River Rhine.

After quizzing the local inhabitants and confirming that, yes, the snow always did melt there first each year, he ordered vineyards to be planted on the hills concerned – and those self-same vineyards (given subsequently to Benedictine monks) still produce some of the greatest of all German wines to this day.

Charlemagne's interest in the project was hardly surprising, because wine-growing had already been firmly entrenched in Germany for the best part of eight centuries . . . and wine-drinking for appreciably longer. Even before Roman legionaries settled in to man the northernmost frontiers of the Empire against the barbarian hordes, the historian Posidanius recorded – in the second century B.C. – that the German tribes drank a good deal of undiluted wine. But it is highly probable that this wine was imported. Julius Caesar visited the Rhineland twice, in 55 B.C. and 53 B.C., and that scrupulous historian would certainly have referred to the local wine-growing, in his writings, if it had existed. As he did not, it seems a pretty safe assumption that the Romans themselves established the first proper Rhine vineyards some years later.

Many present-day technical expressions in the wine industry are of Latin origin, and the wine museum at Speyer, south of Mannheim, has preserved a large range of Roman vintners' tools found in the area, dating back to the first centuries A.D. The tools were of Greek origin — and similar shapes are used in Greece even now.

Once the Romans had gone, however, the really firm establishment of Rhine wines was due — as usual — to the Church. When the early missionaries brought Christianity to the heathen tribes and built churches and monasteries throughout the land, they often had problems in importing the wine essential for celebrating mass. Where conditions were suitable, the local clergy found it safer and cheaper to produce their own wines. Later, following Charlemagne's example, German princes and other nobles got into the habit of storing up goods in heaven by making generous gifts of land to its representatives on earth. These gifts founded the enormous temporal as well as spiritual power which the church enjoyed in Germany from the tenth to the sixteenth centuries. Before long, production from the monastery vineyards far outstripped the monks' own needs and they began to trade in wine — the effective start of the modern industry.

Indeed, the first recorded mentions of such still-renowned vineyards as Eisenach, Geisenheim, Kreuznach and Rudesheim appear as early as the ninth century, and there are references to Nierstein wines towards the end of the tenth century.

The Palatinate

Today, there are four principal districts for the growing of Rhine wines. The largest and southernmost is the

Palatinate, (or *Rheinpfalz* in German) which starts above the Franco-German border and runs up the west bank of the Rhine, along the slopes of the Hardt mountains. The grape chiefly used is the Sylvaner, though the Palatinate's greatest vineyards are given over to the aristocratic Riesling. Among the famous names from this district are Ruppertsberg, Deidesheim, Durkheim and Kallstadt.

Several of the individual vineyards reflect a bizarre local tradition, in that they bear blatantly unpleasant names (but all the easier to remember of course). Among examples are: Sow's Belly *(Saumagen)*, the Monster *(Ungeheur)*, and the Rubbish Tip *(Gerumpel)* — at Kallstadt, Forst and Wachenheim, respectively. Happily, the ugliness of their names is in inverse ratio to the beauty of their wines.

Most Palatinate wines have a higher degree of alcohol and less acidity than those of the other three main districts. Bland yet strong in character, they go well with spicier foods which would overwhelm their lighter, more elegant neighbours.

The Rheinhessen

Immediately north of the Palatinate is the second largest of the Rhine wine districts, Rheinhessen, extending roughly from the ancient city of Worms to the southern bank of the Rhine, where the river runs westwards between Mainz and Bingen. Here again, Sylvaner is the most used grape, with Riesling mainly reserved for the finest locations. Well-known wine names from this district include Alsheim, Guntersblum, Dienheim, Oppenheim, Nierstein and Nackenheim.

Around the last-named, in particular, the region is known for its distinctive bright red sandstone soil, producing wines of charm and mellowness — the basic characteristics of all Liebfraumilch, whose name originated in this district, from the vineyards around the Liebfrauenstift church at Worms. (Initially, in fact, the word was *Liebfrauenminch, minch* being an old German word for monk.)

The Nahe

The Western boundary of Rheinhessen is formed by the River Nahe, which flows into the Rhine at Bingen. On its banks lie vineyards where, records show, wine has been made virtually without break since Roman times. The wines from this third of the Rhine wine districts have much of the lightness and delicate bouquet of the Moselles grown beyond the hills to the west, but also some of the flavour of their own Rhine neighbours to the east. Among the outstanding features of the Nahe district are the rocky red cliffs of Rotenfells, which give out great heat in summer, to the considerable benefit of the vines since the earliest times.

Oddly enough, though, despite the long history of Nahe wines, one of the district's most celebrated vineyards, Schloss Böckelheimer Kupfergrube, is relatively young. It was planted in the last century over an old copper mine — after the undergrowth and rubble had been cleared from the site by convict labour!

The Rheingau

The last of the Rhine wine districts, the Rheingau, lies opposite Rheinhessen on the northern bank of the river – extending approximately from Hochheim in the east to Rudesheim in the west. Although the smallest of the four districts, the Rheingau produces the noblest and most vinous of all Rhine wines — names like Johannisberg, Rudesheim, Steinberg, Geisenheim, Kiedrich, Erbach and Hattenheim. With its vineyards directly open to the warm sun to the south, yet protected from the cold northerly winds by the forests on the upper slopes of the Taunus Mountains, its situation could hardly be bettered.

The great wines of the Rheingau stem almost entirely from the Riesling vine, whose small grapes resist frost well and ripen later, a factor which contributes to the extraordinary variety of bouquets and tastes in the wines.

Moselle

Germany's other main wine region — separate from the four Rhine wine districts but making many wines which have a renown equalled only by the finest hocks — is the Moselle (in German, *Mosel*).

The original Moselle vineyards were laid out by Roman legionaries. The white wines they produce, now grown almost entirely from the aristocratic Riesling grape, are generally lighter than Rhine wines, both in alcohol and colour — the ultra-pale yellows frequently having a faint greenish tint. Unlike hocks, they do not usually improve in bottle and are best drunk somewhat younger (from a year old, or so).

However, Moselles complement hocks rather than rival them. Among their most distinctive qualities are their delicacy, pleasing touch of acidity and gorgeously fragrant bouquets. Because of their refreshing lightness and the dry (but not too dry) characteristics of the best growths, they are wines which can be drunk right through a meal.

Since Roman times, too, they have also had a reputation for health-giving properties, particularly for kidney and similar ailments. One story from the fourteenth century tells how a local archbishop fell ill in his castle at Bernkastel and, when all medical treatment failed, was feared to be on his deathbed; but then a flask of wine was brought to him from one of the neighbouring vineyards and, after drinking it, he made a miraculous recovery. In gratitude, the archbishop renamed the wine 'Bernkasteler Doktor'. Whether or not the story is true, it is certainly a fact that Bernkasteler Doktor acquired international fame after King Edward VII was advised to drink it by his physician. However, to be objective about it, the Doktor wines are actually no better in quality than many other, less expensive Moselles; and it is probable that any medical advantages (perhaps stemming from the potash and salts in the slate-covered soil) are common to most of the top-grade Moselle growths.

The River Moselle itself rises in France's Vosges mountains, flows through Luxembourg, then runs in a general north-easterly direction from the ancient cathedral city of Trier until it joins the Rhine at Coblenz. Just above and below Trier are two small tributaries, the Saar and the Ruwer, both with vineyards producing wines similar to and good enough to be classed as Moselles. The main stretch is divided into three sections, the Upper, Middle and Lower Moselle, with the finest growths coming from the Middle section.

From Trier to Coblenz is a little over 95 kilometres (60 miles), as the crow flies. But the river twists and turns so much that it actually covers about twice that distance, greatly increasing the area available for vineyards. Moreover, because of this winding about, many more vineyards face south, getting more sun than the river's prevailing direction would otherwise have allowed.

The Moselle region is the third most prolific of the German wine-growing areas, yet probably has not more than 10,000 hectares (25,000 acres) under vine. Even though, in many districts, every possible square metre is planted, covering the hills in green, this total area seems a good deal less than one might have expected from the length of the river banks. The explanation is simple: much of the valley is so deep and narrow that the overall width of the wine-growing strip, from its farthest edges on either side of the river, is rarely more than 8 kilometres (5 miles). Most of the vineyards, in fact, are cut in terraces up the hill slopes, often inaccessible by road — and always entailing arduous manual labour to tend them.

One of the most laborious tasks for Moselle wine-growers each year is to break up slabs of slate from the rocks, carry them up the steep steps to the vineyards and scatter the small pieces over the clay topsoil. Despite the barren appearance of the ground, the Riesling stocks thrive in this slate dressing more than in any other. Artificial fertilizers are sometimes used, but still do not seem to have the full advantages of the traditional method.

Besides helping to keep the soil moist, the slate contributes valuable chemicals to the vines as it erodes through the normal processes of wind and weather. It also has the beneficial effect of storing up the warmth of the sun and then reflecting this back on the grapes by night, thus speeding up their ripening.

Broadly speaking, wines from the Upper Moselle, the southernmost section from the Luxembourg border to the mouth of the Saar, are not sufficiently distinguished to be exported. They are either consumed locally or are used for making Sekt, the German white sparkling wine.

From the Saar district, the names most likely to be encountered on wine lists in other countries are from the villages of Ayl, Kanzem, Konz, Ockfen, Wawern, Wiltingen, and the Scharzberg vineyard. The best known Ruwer wines come from Eitelsbach (particularly Karthauserhofberg) and Kasel, plus the outstanding Maximin Grunhauser from the Mertesdorf locality.

The Middle Moselle, extending over some 50 kilometres (30 miles) on a direct line, has about thirty-five villages – each with its own large collection of vineyards. It would be impossible to list all the vineyards here, but the main villages which have achieved world fame for their wines are, from Trier northwards: Longuich, Leiwen, Trittenheim, Neumagen (probably the oldest wine centre in Germany, praised by the Roman poet Ausonius), Dhron, Piesport, Niederemmel, *Brauneberg*, Lieser, Mulheim, Kues, *Bernkastel*, *Graach*, *Wehlen*, *Zeltingen*, *Urzig*, *Erden*, Krov, Traben-Trarbach, Enkirch and Reil.

(Those in italics are regarded as the most distinguished.)

On the northern fringe of the Middle Moselle is Zell, a Roman settlement now known to every German wine-drinker for its wines sold under the generic name of Schwartze Katz (black cat), with unique labels showing a black cat on a wine barrel.

The Lower Moselle, from Bullay to Coblenz, is much like the Upper section in that most of its wines are drunk locally or made into Sekt. However, there are slightly better growths, occasionally exported, from Alf, Cochem, Kern and Winningen.

One of the important features of the Moselle region is that the majority of the vineyards are each shared out among several proprietors. This, coupled with the continual changes in the geographical aspect and other characteristics of the terrain, means that the quality of the wine from a given vineyard is liable to vary considerably, not only from one grower to another, but even between different parts of the stretch owned by a single proprietor. In theory, therefore, while the names of a reputable village and vineyard (or proprietor) on a label are a pretty good guarantee in themselves, the only way to be absolutely sure that the bottle contains their best product is by trial and error.

But in practice, rather than go to this expense, it is wiser to rely on your wine merchant's advice. After all, he in turn is kept constantly informed of the latest 'best buys' by his wholesaler's wine experts, who have already carried out their own extensive tastings before deciding which particular wine to import.

One property common to all the best Moselle and Rhine wines alike is that, the later the grapes are picked, the more their sweetness and other characteristics are enhanced. So the growers leave selected bunches on the vines much longer than usual — sometimes well into November. The words used to describe these better wines, in ascending order of quality, are:

Spätlese – literally 'late gathering'. It is the first gathering after the general harvest, the grapes still being in bunches.

Auslese – specially selected. This gathering is made from fully matured bunches from which all imperfect grapes have been removed.

Beerenauslese – specially selected grapes, usually only in the finest vineyards, which have been allowed to become overripe or affected by the *pourriture noble* (noble rot), a fungus which also helps in the making of the greatest French sweet white wines, such as Sauternes.

Trockenbeerenauslese – the final gathering, made from specially selected dried grapes which have become as shrunken as raisins, giving them a very high concentration of sugar. This concentration, coupled with the essential *pourriture noble,* results in quite exceptional wines which almost have the consistency of liqueurs.

Champagne

For many generations, champagne has been the automatic choice, pocket permitting, for celebrating the principal high spots in our lives – weddings, christenings (and in some cases, perhaps, the prior festivities leading to same. . . .) This doubtless helps to explain why champagne-growers habitually keep up to five years' stock in hand – millions of bottles, stacked in cellars so vast that visitors touring some of them have to do so by miniature underground railway.

True champagne can come only from a rigidly defined region towards the north-east of France. Spreading southwards from Reims, it covers about 30,000 hectares (74,000 acres) of which approximately 20,000 hectares (50,000 acres) are under vine at present. Fossils of vine leaves dating back to prehistoric times have been discovered in the area, so it is probable that the local people knew about wine-making even before the Roman legionaries arrived.

Subsequently, the Church took over where the Romans left off and the vineyards' prosperity was developed by the monasteries. St Remy, the Archbishop of Reims at the end of the fifth century, who began the tradition of crowning the kings of France in Reims Cathedral, mentioned vineyards many times in his will.

In the eleventh century, Pope Urban II, a native of Champagne, had supplies of his own wine from Qy (still one of the greatest champagne-growing centres) brought specially to Rome.

King Henry IV of France was so delighted with the wines from his press-house in the village that he gave himself the title of 'Lord of Ay'. Among other kings who

'Personally I think champagne goes with everything!'

owned press-houses there, later, was England's Henry VIII. Members of the nobility, English as well as French, can be found working for many of the champagne firms to this day.

The earlier royal interest could, on occasion, have its hazards. One account tells how the German Emperor Wenceslas, when he came to Reims in 1398 to discuss affairs of state with Charles VI of France, drank so much that, overcome by fumes of wine, 'he signed everything that was put before him'.

The champagne wines of this period were not the 'bubbly' we know today. While they had a particularly pure, clear quality and were often recommended for medicinal purposes, they consisted of red, white and rosé wines, cousins to the products of Burgundy. A number appear to have shown sparkling characteristics but they never retained them for long.

It was a Benedictine monk, Dom Pérignon, chief cellarer of Haut-villers Abbey, who discovered the secret of capturing their natural effervescence, in the latter half of the seventeenth century. Not only was he the first to control the fermentation, but he also developed the skill of blending wines of different growths, the cuvées, which created a wine that was finer and more delicate in its ensemble than any of its components.

Many scientific improvements have been made since then in the production of champagne — notably under the urging of Napoleon, after a visit to the region in 1807. Special bottles were manufactured, with the right power of resistance. New, better ways of using the cork stopper were found. Modern science also plays an even bigger part in cultivation, blending and other processes. But we can still thank the basic rules laid down by Dom Pérignon for making it all possible.

Nowadays, champagne can be made only from three 'noble' vine stocks: the Pinot Noir and the Pinot Meunier, both with black grapes but yielding white wine, and the elegant white Chardonnay. These are the vines, which, from more than 1000 years' experience, have proved best suited to the region's soil and climate — the two factors directly responsible for champagne's unique personality.

Planted in a covering of fertile earth up to 50 centimetres (20 inches) deep, the vine roots spread into a thick layer of limestone. The chalky subsoil allows excess water to seep through, while preserving sufficient humidity in the soil itself. It also has the advantage of storing up and reflecting the warmth of the sun, to the great appreciation of the ripening plants.

Another advantage of the chalk is that it is easily dug, so it has been possible to make cellars out of chalk-pits and galleries which have existed since Roman times. Altogether, these cellars now stretch for more than 190 kilometres (120 miles), some of them as deep as 45 metres (150 feet) below the surface. With the nearby forests helping to regulate the variations of moisture, the cellars maintain an average daily temperature throughout the year of 10° C (50° F), which is exactly right for the champagne-making process.

Picking of the grapes begins towards the end of September. Each bunch is carefully examined, skilled sorters rejecting all imperfect grapes, In large baskets, holding about 70 kilos (150 pounds) at a time, they are brought in from the vineyards and emptied into large, shallow wine-presses, each holding about 4 tonnes of grapes, from which 2700 litres (596 gallons) of juice are produced. Any juice obtained in excess of that amount is not allowed to become champagne. The pressing is carried out quickly, as that the juice does not have time to become red through contact with the skins of the black grapes. Running from the presses into vats, the juice is pumped into 200-litre (45-gallon) barrels and transported to the cellars of the champagne houses, where the first fermentation takes place, turning the grape sugar into alcohol. This lasts several weeks, eventually producing a still white wine. After being exposed to colder temperatures and racked several times to make it absolutely clear and stable, the wine is tasted by the champagne house's own specialists, to determine its specific qualities, and it is then blended with ten or twenty others to make up a cuvée – ensuring continuity of taste and 'house style'.

If it is a very good year, the blending is confined to wines of the same harvest, to produce a vintage vine with its own distinct personality.

Next, small quantities of cane sugar and fermenting agents are added, and the wine is bottled and placed to rest in the cellars, where a second fermentation occurs in bottle. This time, the sparkle is born – the sugar being turned into alcohol and carbonic gas, which stays imprisoned in the bottle.

During the fermentation, which takes several months to complete, a deposit forms on the lower side of the bottles. To clear this deposit, the bottles are placed neck downwards, in tilted racks. Every other day, for some months more, a cellarman gives each bottle a slight twist and progressively increases the tilt until at last the bottle is nearly vertical, cork down. This procedure, called the *remuage*, makes the deposit slide slowly into the neck and collect around the inner end of the cork.

Next – and not for a year or perhaps several years – comes the *dégorgement* (disgorging), when the neck of the bottle is dipped into a freezing solution, forming a small block of ice which contains the deposit. When an operator extracts the cork, the internal pressure ejects the ice block and, with it, the unwanted deposit.

Lastly, the clear wine is topped up with a small 'dosage' of grape sugar, the precise amount depending on the degree of sweetness desired, i.e. whether the champagne is to be extra-dry, dry, or demi-sec (sweet). Then a new cork is inserted and held in place by a strong wire cage. On goes the gold foil round the neck and that precious champagne label . . . *et voilà!* Hats off to old Dom Pérignon!

Other sparkling wines

Champagne is, by universal consent, the greatest sparkling wine – and many people tend to regard all other sparkling wines as lesser alternatives whose main asset is simply that they are somewhat cheaper than the 'real thing'. However, though these others certainly do have an advantage on price, it would not be doing them justice to buy them for that reason alone. A great number of them deserve to stand on their own feet and be appraised as very good wines in their own right.

These other sparkling wines may be related to champagne – anything from first cousins to third cousins twice removed – but they are quite distinct from it. While they may be made by the same method used by the growers of Reims and Epernay, they can never be quite the same, if only because of the wide variations in soil, climate and the grapes used. After all, sparkling wines are produced in many different regions of France, in Germany, Italy, Spain, Portugal, Australia, America . . . in fact, almost anywhere that people make wine. Obviously, therefore, local conditions vary enormously – and the wines likewise.

You may meet those from Germany under the general title of Sekt (or perhaps Sparkling Hock and Sparkling Moselles); those from Italy as one or other of the Spumante wines (e.g. Asti); while the Spanish sparkling wines are *vinos espumosos* – though your holiday waiter may be in the habit (illicitly, of course) of referring to them as 'champan'.

Wherever they come from, though, all the better-class sparkling wines are made in one of three different ways: (1) the traditional *méthode champenoise*, involving a secondary fermentation in bottle, as I described in the previous section on champagne. Because of the time and labour required, sparkling wines made by this method are bound to cost more than other versions. At the same time, however, from the painstaking care implicit in the method, it is fair to say that these are virtually always the best sparkling wines.

(2) The transfer system, which differs from the *méthode champenoise* principally in that, instead of removing the sediment by the *remuage* method after its secondary fermentation, the wine is transferred by means of a sealed circuit to a pressurized holding tank. The sediment settles in the tank, and the wine is drawn off and filtered before being put into new bottles.

(3) The cuve close — a cheaper and quicker method, but still capable of producing first-rate wines. With this system, the crucial secondary fermentation does not take place in bottle; it is carried out instead in large glass-lined concrete or stainless steel tanks. The tanks are completely sterile, all contact with the air being excluded. Temperature, sugar additions and so on can be controlled very precisely, cutting out the long period of maturing needed with the 'champagne method' and enabling the wines to be produced in a few months.

While found particularly in Italy and Germany, the cuve close has been adopted by increasing numbers of firms in pretty well all countries where sparkling wines are made.

To try to give a list of the best sparkling wines is a somewhat invidious task. For a start, I haven't tasted them *all*! So perhaps the best way is to concentrate solely on the main European types which you can usually find at your wine merchants.

France

It is generally accepted that, other than champagne, the best French sparkling wines (*vins mousseux*) are those made in the Saumur district on the River Loire. The industry there was founded early in the nineteenth century by a Belgian who had studied in the Champagne region and who realized that the miles of deep chalk caves in the hills by Saumur (and often extending right under the town itself) provided ideal conditions for the long, natural process of the *méthode champenoise*. Although different local grape varieties are used, the sparkling wines of highest quality from the district are still made by this method.

Sizeable quantities of good sparkling wines are also made in the Bordeaux and Burgundy regions. Sparkling red burgundy became a very fashionable export during the Gay Nineties and Edwardian times. Though no longer such a fad, you can still come across it here and there. And I do not go along with those pundits who regard it as overrated. To my mind, it is always interesting to drink something slightly out of the ordinary, if only occasionally — and it can still be very impressive when you're entertaining a pretty girl!

Germany

The word Sekt simply means a German sparkling wine and can cover a very wide range of tastes and qualities. It is nearly always white, though some red sparkling wines are also made; it may be sparkling hock or sparkling Moselle; it can be extremely sweet or quite dry; it may be based on pretty ordinary, cheap wines or in blends with imported wines, or on wines from Germany's greatest vineyards.

How the word was first adopted makes a good yarn. It seems that there was an old Berlin tavern where the deriders invariably broke into smiles when the actor Ludwig Devrient came in for a drink after his evening performance at the royal theatre. Without fail, he would quote from his role as Falstaff by calling out in round Shakespearean terms: 'Hey, villain, bring,me a cup of sack.' Equally without fail, the waiter made no attempt to serve sherry, which is what Falstaff was actually ordering; instead, he brought the actor's unvarying tipple, champagne.

When Shakespeare's plays were first translated into German, the word 'sack' was rendered as *sekt* – and for more than 150 years, this was used in Germany to denote a still Spanish wine. But after Ludwig Devrient began perpetrating his tavern joke in 1815, his personal definition caught on and, in Berlin at any rate, Sekt came to mean any sparkling wine.

That is the story told by one of the wine industry's most distinguished figures, S.F. Hallgarten; and it is certainly true that, by the 1830s, the old meaning of *sekt* had disappeared and Ludwig's interpretation was in general use throughout the country. By then, too, a number of German wine-growers had returned home after working with French champagne firms at Reims and had laid the foundations of a sparkling wine industry which now produces Sekt in virtually every West German wine-growing centre. There are about 125 Sekt firms throughout the country, of which nearly thirty produce more than a million bottles each annually. You get some idea of the industry's size when you realize that the annual production of Sekt, in numbers of bottles, is roughly twice that of champagne.

While Sekt can be made from almost any blend of grapes suitable for the purpose, the best are based on Germany's finest grape, the Riesling, producing dryish white wines which are noted for their fruitiness and attractive bouquet. Some of the finest of all come from single great-name estates, such as Steinberg and Johannisberg. Provided at least two-thirds of the wine used in making it was grown on the estate concerned, the Sekt is entitled to bear the vineyard's name.

A small amount of the best Sekt is still made by the *méthode champenoise*, (as it was by the pioneers who learned their trade at Reims). But earlier prejudice against the cuve close or the tank system has largely disappeared – partly because of the close scientific control which it permits and partly because of the improvements which have been introduced in recent years. For instance, scientists have developed new filtration processes, said to be superior to the traditional *dégorgement* by hand.

As a result, many German firms claim that they can now produce Sekt by the tank system which is almost indistinguishable in quality from that made by the 'champagne method'.

Italy

By far the best known Italian sparkling wine is Asti Spumante, made in the Piedmont region (by the cuve close method) from Muscat grapes which give it a sweet and highly distinctive scented taste. Partly because of this characteristic flavour, and partly because of its low alcoholic strength, it has long been a popular wine for all members of the family.

There are also many other drier sparkling wines, made by leading firms, which are not entitled to the name Asti and are usually sold under brand names. Among further Italian 'sparklers' are the red Nebbiolo Spumante and the very dry Gran Spumante, made from the Pinot grape by the 'champagne method'.

Spain

When foreign tourists in Spain order a bottle of champagne in that last mad fling at the end of their holiday (or any other occasion, for that matter), the waiter will bring them a bottle which has all the traditional trimmings – gold foil round the neck, wired cork, and so on – and which he will call 'champan' without any hesitation.

But the odds are that it isn't. That is, not if you mean the sparkling wine grown in France's Champagne region, which is the only wine legally entitled to bear the name. Unless you are rich enough to buy the imported genuine article, which is taxed very highly, the 'champan' sold in Spain is entirely a home-grown product. However, this need not spoil the holidaymaker's pleasure. Many of Spain's sparkling wines *(vinos espumosos)* are first-rate products, carefully made and eminently drinkable.

The Spanish sparkling wine industry was founded just over a century ago in the little town of San Sadurni de Noya, 40 kilometres (25 miles) west of Barcelona — by the head of a family which had been making normal table wines in the area since 1551. Today, it is claimed that the huge cellars at San Sadurni de Noya are nearly twice the size of any other cellars in the world. That may be an exaggeration — I wouldn't know — but certainly they are by far the biggest cellars in Spain.

Sparkling wines are also produced in fair quantities in the north-westerly provinces adjoining the Portuguese border, in the famed Rioja district (home of Spain's greatest table wines) and as far north as Spain's Mediterranean border with France.

However, the two most important districts both lie within easy reach of the holiday centres north and south of Barcelona. To the north, hugging the Costa Brava, is the Alella district — a hilly area familiar to tourists for its fields of carnations but known above all for its white wines. Those produced in the coastal zone tend to have greater alcoholic strength, less acidity and a more pronounced bouquet than the white wines made in the district's central and high altitude zones inland, though it is the latter which make the best sparkling wines.

The Alella vineyards, incidentally, are among the oldest in the country, planted originally by Phoenicians and Greek settlers about 600 B.C., or even earlier.

South of Barcelona is the Panades district, familiar to

holidaymakers in such places as Sitges. It is similar in climate and soil to Alella but has a much bigger vineyard area. The vineyards of the High Panades are some of the highest in Spain, lying at an altitude of nearly 700 metres (2300 feet). San Sadurni de Noya, the sparkling wine 'capital', is lower down in the Central Panades, about 24 kilometres (15 miles) due north of Sitges. Several other townships hereabouts also have a thriving trade in such wines. Although I haven't been there myself, I'm told that those worth visiting include San Esteban de Sas Roviras, Pla del Panades and La Granada (not to be confused with the famous Moorish city in the far south of Spain).

By the nature of the process, the best quality sparkling wines will normally be those made by the 'champagne method'. About forty Spanish firms still use the method and they are the only ones officially allowed to describe themselves as *cavas* (equivalent to the French *caves* — wine cellars). They are deservedly proud of their products and are almost always willing to show visitors round the premises. So if you are on holiday in Spain and get the chance to see one of these *cavas*, please don't miss it. You'll find it a fascinating experience.

Hints on serving

Champagne and all other sparkling wines should be served cool but not iced. The best way is to cool the bottle in a pail half filled with ice and water. If you use a refrigerator, put the bottle in the main compartment — *never* in the freezer.

When opening the bottle, always wrap a cloth round it. After removing the coil and wire cage, hold the bottle at an angle of 45° away from you and then grasp the cork firmly with one hand while rotating the bottle with the other, i.e. you twist the bottle round the cork. That way, the cork comes out easily and you can withdraw it bit by bit, allowing the gas to escape slowly, without causing a loud 'pop'. The explosive noise may be exciting but it would horrify the cellarmen of Reims and Epernay. *Their* proud boast is always to withdraw the cork with a soft 'thw'tt'. *Never* use a swizzle-stick. Why bother to drink champagne if you start by getting rid of bubbles that took years to put there?

Rosé wines

Ask any wine waiter what a newcomer to wine-drinking is most likely to order, when dining out, and it's odds on that he'll answer: 'A rosé'. The reason that rosé (i.e. pink) wines are so popular in this context, I suppose, is that they represent a perfect compromise. . . . Certainly, they seem to offer a safe half-way choice between red and white wines, in taste as well as colour. But they are not only an easy escape from the puzzlements of a long wine list. Suppose you've taken a small party to a restaurant and your guests' choices for their main course range from lobster to steak; in such a case — if you don't want to buy more than one bottle of wine — a rosé appears to be an ideal solution.

Some of the more pompous wine pundits might disagree with such expedients. Oddly enough, though, they give an impression of being rather shy of the subject. Many weighty books about wine touch only briefly on the various rosés, then sheer away quickly. One writer, for instance, dismisses them as being 'a pleasant accompaniment to the kind of meal at which nobody is going to pay much attention to the wine.' Yet this is one case, in my view, when the amateur's commonsense attitude has more right on its side. For a start, nobody questions that rosés *do* go well with most food. Because they are usually drunk chilled, they go best with lighter dishes — but they *can* be drunk right through a meal.

Again, while they have nowhere near the depth, long-lasting qualities and almost endless variety of top-class red and white wines, there are nevertheless distinct differences between specific rosé wines which are well worth appreciating.

One of the most widespread misconceptions about rosés, even on the Continent, concerns the method of producing them. Many people still think they are made simply by blending red and white wines. It *can* be done that way, but the result is not so good.

In fact, all the better class rosés are made from black grapes, and growers set out to make them quite deliberately. With the best rosés, as for any other good wines, their methods try to achieve continuity of style and standard from one year to the next. So there is nothing haphazard about it.

All wine comes from the natural fermentation of juice obtained by pressing ripe grapes. The juice, or 'must', begins to rumble away furiously within a matter of hours and the fermenting may take several weeks to complete; the resultant wine is then matured quietly in cask – for many years, in some cases – until it is ready for bottling.

Between the production of red and white wines, however, there is one salient difference. Red wines are made from black grapes, which are pressed in their entirety, including the skins, and sometimes even the stalks. White wines are made from red or white grapes, and the juice passes into the fermenting casks *without* the skins. (Because the colour is in the skins, it is possible to produce white wine from black grapes – as happens with 80 % of champagne – provided the black skins are removed before the fermentation.)

To produce rosé wines, the black grape skins are left in contact with the 'must' for a short, calculated period, generally twelve to twenty-four hours, thus imparting a little of their colour to the fermenting juice. The longer the period, the darker the colour – which is why rosés range from deep, almost coppery hues down to only the faintest pinkish tinge.

That is only a broad description of a complex process

which has many variations and refinements, but it gives a fair idea. After this initial stage, a rosé is made like a white wine, which means that it is generally ready for bottling much earlier than most red wines. The majority of rosés are dry to medium-dry in taste.

In a very few areas, the growers follow a different method, obtaining the 'must' for their rosés from a judicious mixture of black and white grapes. (Not at all the same thing as mixing red and white wines together, of course.) The most notable of these exceptions is Tavel, probably the best of all French rosés, grown in vineyards west of Avignon, across the river from the famous Châteauneuf du Pape vineyards. More than a million bottles of Tavel rosés are produced each year. The wine is drier than most other rosés and has more character and body.

Another distinguished French rosé comes from the Anjou district, cradle of England's Plantagenet kings, south of the River Loire. This is Cabernet Rosé, somewhat sweeter than Tavel and lighter in colour. Altogether, some 4000 hectares (10,000 acres) of Anjou's vineyards — a quarter of the total — are devoted to the production of rosés, yielding more than 13 million litres (3 million gallons) annually.

The other local rosés, pleasant, but of lesser stature than Cabernet, share one unusual feature with it: they are all traditionally served in a long-stemmed glass, with a flat-bottomed, straight-sided bowl, which is used for no other French wine.

However, the production of rosé wines is scattered throughout nearly every wine-growing country, albeit often in small quantities. In France herself, besides Tavel and Anjou, local rosés can be found from Alsace, in the far north-east, to the Bearn region south of Pau, approaching the Pyrenees in the south-west of the country. From the other end of the Pyrenees, stretching around the Mediterranean shore towards the mouth of the Rhône west of Marseilles, come the simple, refreshing rosés of Languedoc-Roussillon.

Some 30 kilometres (20 miles) the other side of Marseilles, approaching the French Riviera, is the home of the Côtes de Provence rosés — a wealth of good little wines, tending to be sweeter than most other rosés.

Moving northwards, beautiful rosés are made in the vineyards of Lirac and Chuscian, adjoining the great Tavel itself; and north-eastwards across the Rhône, others becoming popular with tourists are produced around the wonderfully named township of Vinsobres.

To the north again, through the ultra-pale rosés of the Beaujolais district, with a look across to the French Alps and the mountain rosés of Savoie, and then past the westernmost tip of Switzerland, we come to another famous centre for these wines, the Jura. Here is a second region in which the best rosés are made by pressing black and white grapes at the same time. The Jura rosés, lively and fresh, and sometimes with a hint of sparkle, gradually acquire a bronze gleam known as *pelure d'oignon* ('onion skin') — and that's the name by which you order them in Paris bistros.

Indeed, it is hard to think of a single corner of France where rosés cannot be found, though many of them seldom leave their own localities.

They are pretty prolific, too, in several other countries. Among those sold abroad are rosés from Switzerland (including one called 'Partridge Eye'); from Yugoslavia (the traditional Ruzica of Serbia); from Cyprus (the very dark Kokineli); even a sparkling rosé from Russia — but above all from Spain and Portugal, where rosés are made in virtually every wine-growing area.

Some Spanish rosés are full and powerful; others, particularly from the Panades district south of Barcelona, are sparkling; a few styles were probably being made in Roman times. However, one of the most extraordinary success stories of recent years has been the enormous growth in demand for sparkling rosé imported from Portugal. In its unusual flat-sided bottles — most rosés are sold in hock-style bottles — this refreshing wine comes principally from a district adjoining the Douro (where port is made) in northern Portugal. Should you be holidaying in Portugal, you will find many more rosés throughout the length and breadth of the country. One particularly worth taking a trip to experience is the Faisca rosé from Setubal, the peninsula on the opposite side of the Tagus from Lisbon.

With such variety of rosé wines, from these and numerous other wine-growing countries, it remains only to recall that there is even a rosé version of champagne. So-called pink champagne — properly known as champagne rosé — is made by adding to the white 'bubbly' a little red champagne wine, produced from black grapes. These come mostly from the vineyards of Bouzy and Trepail. Bouzy? An apt name, indeed.

Fortified wines

Here's a teaser once put to me by a friend in the wine trade: to which different types of wine do the following descriptions refer, and what special characteristics do they have in common?

1. Although made since Roman times, if not earlier, it owes its real discovery to British merchants, as recently as the eighteenth century.
2. It has been exported widely for more than 700 years – thanks initially to the explusion of the Moors from Europe.
3. It is the longest-living wine in the world.

The answers, respectively, are: port, sherry and madeira. And the characteristic they share is that all are fortified wines. That is, at some stage of their production, they are strengthened by the addition of brandy or wine spirit, making them about twice as strong as table wines (and in turn, about half the strength of standard grades of spirits like brandy, whisky and gin).

Besides those already cited, two other fortified wines still exported, though less generally familiar, are Malaga, from Spain, and Marsala, from Sicily. The Malaga region, on the Mediterranean coast east of Gibraltar, is a leading package-holiday centre and many holidaymakers are now rediscovering its rich, sweet dessert wines. These were actually in public favour long before sherry, but for some time have been used mostly in other countries as an ingredient of sauces and for similiar cooking purposes.

Marsala dessert wines take their name from that of a Sicilian port and the surrounding district, which the Arab invaders called Mars al Allah, meaning 'the port of God'. The pleasant, nutty flavour of the wines greatly attracted Nelson, when he was introduced to them on his triumphant return from the Battle of the Nile, and he ordered large quantities for his sailors. But latterly, like Malaga, Marsala has tended to have a mainly culinary emphasis abroad. So I shall concentrate only on the three best known.

Sherry

'If I had a thousand sons, the first human principle I would teach them should be — to forswear thin potations and to addict themselves to sack'. That was Shakespeare's Falstaff talking about the wine we know today as sherry . . . and it would seem that the little bit of Falstaff lurking in the hearts of most English-speaking people has readily taken his advice, for sherry remains by far the most popular of all fortified wines.

The only wine which may be described by the single word 'sherry', without qualifying it by its country of origin, comes from a relatively small area in the far south of Spain. Centre of this strictly delimited region, in which barely 98 square kilometres (38 square miles) are under vine, is the little white-washed city of Jerez de la Frontera – only 14 kilometres (9 miles) from Cadiz, as the crow flies, though a good deal longer by road round the harbour from which Drake captured some 3000 butts of sherry when he 'singed the King of Spain's beard' in 1587.

The city was probably founded about 1100 B.C. by the Phoenicians. Later it was settled by the Greeks, who called it Xera, then captured by the Carthaginians and finally conquered in 206 B.C. by the Romans, who named it Ceret. The design of some Roman mosaics found there in modern times includes vine leaves and tendrils. But it was many centuries before the local wine found its way farther afield.

Although there is documentary proof of shipments to Britain as early as the twelfth century, the fame of Jerez – which Spain's Moorish occupiers pronounced as 'Sheris' - – was not really established until Alfonso the Wise built a frontier fortress at the city in 1264, to defend the Christians against the Moors. Erection of these frontier defences (whence the city's full name of Jerez de la Frontera) permitted much more land to be extended under vine, and in turn gave rise to the production of *vinos de saca* (wines for export). From this name we derived first the word 'sack' and later from Jerez, the word 'sherry'.

While the production area covers nearly all vineyards in the province of Cadiz, the region for maturing and shipping sherry is confined strictly to three small municipal districts: Jerez itself and the coastal townships of Puerto de Santa Maria and Sanlucar de Barrameda. The vinegrowing soil, in turn, is classified in three distinct types.

The best sherries come from a very white type of soil called *albariza*, an evenly textured mixture of chalk and lime, often containing up to 80 % of calcium carbonate. This produces the highest quality wine, and although its yield is less than from the lower quality soils, modern methods of viticulture produce yields up to 9000 litres per hectare (800 gallons per acre).

A second type of soil, *barro*, darker in colour and usually found on lower ground, produces wines of somewhat lesser quality but has an appreciably bigger yield. The third type, *arena*, largely consisting of sand, gives the highest yield of all; but the wines, again, are of a lesser quality and are used entirely for the production of sweet varieties.

For the sherry grower, not a month goes by without some essential job to be done. His annual routine begins in October with the *deserpia*, when a pit about a metre square is dug round each vine, to direct the autumn rain to the roots. After the first rains, the new ground is levelled off and the soil analysed to find the most suitable vine stock. Then it is manured and marked out, ready for planting the new stocks towards the end of January. Light hoeing follows in February or March; then deeper hoeing to a depth of 20 centimetres (8 inches), to keep down the weeds, in April and early May. Throughout this period, too, there is frequent pruning and tidying of the vines. In May and June, the vines are protected against diseases by spraying with sulphur and with a mixture of copper sulphate and slaked lime. The same two months bring the blossom, followed by the first appearance of the grapes.

During August, when the grapes are slowly ripening and there is less activity in the vineyards, the opportunity is taken to make the graftings for future crops, the sherry-producing vines being grafted on to American stocks or plants, which are resistant to the dreaded disease of phylloxera.

Finally, in mid-September, the harvest begins. Bunches of grapes are dried in the sun on esparto grass mats outside the lagars — the open tanks where the grapes are pressed. Until recent times, the pressing was done by foot — four human treaders per lagar, wearing special hide boots studded with angled nails. But nowadays mechanical presses have been perfected which do the job more efficiently, overcoming the old prejudices against machinery.

The harvest lasts about a month. Then back to the *deserpia* and the whole routine all over again. . . .

It takes five years for a newly grafted vine to yield a useful crop, after which the vine has a productive life of twenty-five to thirty years. Of the great many species of vine cultivated, the variety most commonly used is the Palomino, its sweet medium-sized grapes accounting for 90 % of total sherry production. Next in order of importance is the even sweeter Pedro Ximenez, named after a soldier who brought it back from Germany in the sixteenth century; it is used principally for making a sweet wine for blending purposes.

In the initial stages, no one can tell for sure which type of sherry will emerge from any given crop. The three main types are: Finos (dryest, finest and lightest in colour); Amontillados (really belonging to the Fino types, but becoming nuttier in flavour and more amber-like in colour as they mature); and Olorosos (aromatic, full-bodied, darker in colour).

Yet until the later stages of production, the result is in the laps of the gods. Grapes from the same vineyard may be pressed simultaneously, forming two butts of 'must' which are then taken into town at the same time and stored side by side; they will have been handled in an identical manner, yet it is quite likely that they will mature in completely different ways, one maturing into a Fino and the other into an Oloroso!

Within six hours or so of the pressing, the 'must' begins its tumultuous fermentation and the butts are promptly carried into town to one of the bodegas — the airy, cathedral-like cellars, on ground level, where sherry is matured.

Fermentation lasts two or three months, during which a whitish film known as the *flor* (or 'flower') will appear

69

naturally on the surface of the wine in many butts, preventing direct contact between the air and the young sherry, helping to give the Fino sherries their delicacy and dryness. Once the *flor* has fulfilled its functions, it turns into a brown sediment, leaving a clean wine. Subsequently, the wines are classified and fortified by the addition of alcohol, its strength depending on the sherry's classification.

Each cask is matured separately for a while as *vino de anada*, the wine of a particular year. However, there are hardly any 'vintage' sherries, in the way that a great French wine is known for its best years. This is because of the final, most unusual characteristic of sherry — the fact that, if slightly younger wine of the same type is added to a cask of sherry, it will gradually take on the quality of the older wine. After a few months, the wine in the cask will be indistinguishable from its original contents.

This unique trait makes possible the *solera* system, through which a sherry's consistency of style and quality can be maintained year after year. A *solera* consists of anything from five to fifteen sets of casks of sherry, of the same style but in ascending order of age. Each set of casks in the series is known as a scale.

Two or three times a year, according to demand, a maximum of 25 % of the contents will be withdrawn from the first scale, holding the oldest wine. This is replaced with an equivalent amount from the next scale, a year or two younger; the second cask is refreshed with wine from the third — and so on right up to the last scale, which is refreshed with wine from the *criadera*, or nursery, where all young sherries are kept during their early years of maturing. The complete operation is termed 'running the scales'. Since the final solera product becomes, after a while, identical to the superior old sherry originally contained in the first scale, the shipper can offer it as a standard line *ad infinitum*. When it reaches your wine merchant's shelves, therefore, you can be sure that each and every bottle of your favourite brand of solera sherry — at whatever interval you buy them — will always have precisely the same high quality, the same style, colour, taste and bouquet.

'Other' sherries

Besides the real thing from Spain, several other countries make sherry-style wines which, to ensure the distinction is maintained, must by law always bear the name of the country concerned in front of the word 'sherry'.

You can find very good versions from Cyprus and Australia, for instance. But the one which probably has the biggest sales — and certainly the most unusual story behind it — comes from South Africa.

It is rare indeed for people to be able to identify exactly who was responsible for 'fathering' an entirely new industry — and virtually unique for such a man to be still alive in our own day. But that can certainly be said of Dr Charles Niehaus, a one-time university don whose experiments first made possible the production of South African sherry. Those experiments took place only a few years before the last world war, when Dr Niehaus was still in his twenties. Today, South African sherry is sold all over the world.

Wine has been made at the Cape, within 160 kilometres (100 miles) or so of Cape Town, for more than three centuries. The original vines were planted in 1655 by Jan van Riebeeck, commander of the first Dutch settlement sent out to establish a half-way station on the trade route to the East Indies. On 2 February 1659 he recorded in his diary: 'Today — God be praised — wine was made for the first time from Cape grapes.'

Twenty years later, his successor as Governor of the Dutch colony, Simon van der Stel, took things a stage further by growing the Cape's first really fine wines on his farm at Groot Constantia (named after his wife,

Constance). Then, in 1688, he gave a welcome to 200 Huguenot immigrants who had fled from France after the revocation of the Edict of Nantes. The refugees, skilled in wine-growing traditions already centuries old, rapidly extended and improved the Cape's vineyards. They also founded the town of Paarl, in a mountain valley 58 kilometres (36 miles) inland from Cape Town, which is now the headquarters of the South African wine industry. But it was not until 1933 that the Cape wine industry began its biggest-ever success story. Early that year, Dr Niehaus returned from wine studies in Europe to his post as Senior Lecturer in Viticulture-Oenology at Stellenbosch University. During his three-year tour, on a government scholarship, he had carried out research work in the Rhine wine region and visited all the main European wine-growing areas, paying special attention to the making of sherry in Spain.

On his return home, he started laboratory tests to explore the possibilities of developing the production of South African sherries. The crucial discovery he made was that the *flor* wine yeast, until then thought to exist only in Spain, was also present in the Cape. This discovery meant that the way was open for growth of top-class South African sherry on a major scale – provided a proper system of maturing the wine could be perfected. And the method chosen was the traditional Spanish *solera* system, described in the previous section.

There was good reason for selecting it, because many of the local conditions of topography and climate in the Cape were remarkably similar to those in Spain. The sandstone soils in the south-western Cape were ideal for producing the pale, more delicate types of sherry; farther east, soils with a high calcium content were suitable for producing fuller types. Even the geographical locations corresponded closely enough to give the right period of sun and rain. Jerez, centre of the Spanish sherry industry, lies on latitude 36.41° north. Paarl is on latitude 33.45°

south; and their weather cycles are almost identical.

The grapes used for making South African sherries are the sweet, medium-sized Palomino (as used for 90 % of Spain's total sherry production); and the Steen, an adaptation of some of the vines planted by the original Dutch pioneers 300 years ago. Some of the soils inevitably differ from those of Jerez; likewise, the Cape *flor* does not always form with the same degree of reliability, so it is cultivated separately and then introduced to the wine. But in nearly all other respects, South African sherrymaking is carried out as closely to the Spanish pattern as possible.

Port

It is fair to say that, without the British, port would probably not have existed. At least, not as we know it today. Port did not really begin to take hold in Britain until after the Methuen Treaty of 1703, which granted Customs preference to Portuguese wines, in a deliberate bid to 'dish' the French wines trade. However, the original port wines — much thinner and less attractive than the velvety treasures now familiar to us — had been known abroad for many centuries before that. Throughout the Middle Ages, they had reached England mainly through the barter trade normal in that period for two friendly maritime nations, with Portuguese wines being exchanged for English woollens and similar goods.

Even before the Methuen Treaty, a fair number of British merchants had already settled in Portugal during the latter half of the seventeenth century, realizing the opportunities presented by the increasing hostilities with France. The merchants came from Devon, Yorkshire, London, and especially from Scotland, as shown by many of the company names renowned in the trade to this day — Cockburn, Croft, Graham, Sandeman, Taylor.

It was they who seized on the possibilities of popularizing the local wines back home; but, despite the open door offered by the 1703 treaty, the port was still only a run-of-the-mill product — and it was not until one of the shippers added a little brandy spirit to his port exports that new prospects began to emerge. The shipper's object had been simply to help his product withstand the difficult sea voyage to England. It was found, though, that the added spirit did not merely keep the wine in good condition but actually made it taste much better, in itself. A classic case of serendipity, in fact. . . .

Even so, many people frowned on the practice, and it was years before the addition of brandy became general, turning port into the 'fortified' wine that we drink nowadays. Still more years passed before shippers appreciated the importance of cylindrical glass bottles for holding their port while it matured. Previously, the brandy-fortified port was kept in wooden casks for much longer than was good for it. Only by gradual experiment was it established that port reached its best if it were held in cask for not more than two years or so and then transferred into bottles to mature in peace. As a result, the first great vintage port, as we now understand it, was not declared until 1775.

Even in 'ordinary' years, strict measures of quality are imposed. Port wines can come only from a rigidly defined area, covering about 2000 square kilometres (900 square miles), along the banks of the River Douro, in Northern Portugal. A government body, aided by shippers' and farmers' associations, exercises strong control over every stage — from the initial output permitted to approval of the final product.

One operation carried out under particularly close official control is the blending of ports from several different years and several different vineyards — a highly skilled task which ensures that a port blend is consistent in colour, taste and all other aspects, from one year to the next.

Port, usually a sweet wine, comes in two standard

versions: the deep red *ruby* and the somewhat browner *tawny*, which is rather more dry in taste. Though much less well known outside Portugal itself, you may also find *white* ports, some of which can be quite dry.

Up the scale, two other kinds are *vintage* and *crusted* port. The former is a wine of exceptional quality, declared by individual growers only in very good years. The latter is a blend from two or more vintages. However, it has all but disappeared, and becoming more popular instead is *late-bottled vintage port*. This is kept in cask longer than usual and so comes to maturity more quickly than a traditional vintage port which is matured in bottle for many years.

In recent years, the trade has set out to show that port is not just a drink for stuffy old colonels but one which everybody can enjoy. As the Scottish chairman of one world-renowned port firm put it: 'People used to smile at those pre-war charwomen whose favourite tipple was port and lemon, but the old dears knew a thing or two'. Besides being a superb drink on its own, port is also an excellent 'mixer'. Port and Pepsi, port on the rocks, port and vodka — its versatility is almost endless.

The French, in particular, were quick to realize this. Uninhibited by tradition, they drink port freely as an *apéritif*, a pre-meal appetizer. As a result, France has now overtaken Britain as port's biggest export market.

Nevertheless, the role performed by the old British family firms remains paramount. From their headquarters in Oporto's eighteenth-century Factory House, they remain jealous guardians of port's finest traditions. At the same time, they have been in the forefront of modern innovations, wherever beneficial.

Some customs simply defy change. The men bringing in the big vintage baskets from the rocky vineyards, each basket holding 60 kilograms (130 pounds) of grapes or more, still carry them on their backs with the support of a leather band across their foreheads. On approaching journey's end, they let loose wild wolf-howls — just to show they have plenty of breath left – before tipping their grapes into the lagar, the great tank in which the fruit is pressed.

Because of the schistous soil in which the vines grow, in narrow terraces clinging to the mountain slopes, it is virtually impossible to use such mechanical appliances as tractors. One businessman, who thought his machines could do the job, made a journey to the area for the first time. Emerging from the station, he took one look at the precarious steepness of the terraces, then turned on his heel immediately and asked the time of the next train back to Oporto. . . .

On the other hand, several laborious customs have been dropped readily enough, once it was proved that modern aids were more efficient. For centuries, it was held inviolate that nothing could compare with the human foot for pressing the grapes. The sensitive foot never broke the pips, and the rise and fall of the leg provided the right amount of aeration needed for the 'must' (the grape juice). But now, without any fuss, machines have been introduced which perform the operation just as effectively — and which cut labour requirements from perhaps forty men at a time to only one man in charge of the controls.

Conservative they may be, those British shippers in the Factory House, with their priceless collection of Wedgwood china, their forty-two-place dining table covered with a single damask cloth, and their adjoining, identical room to which they adjourn after the meal for the serious business of savouring the port. Yet, in their devotion to the past, present and future of port, nobody could be more forward looking when it comes to ensure the best interests of the one subject which unites them all . . . As one distinguished managing director habitually put it, after each meal in the Factory House: 'Now that we've got through this tedious part of eating, let's get down to dinner!'

> Have some Madeira, m'dear,
> You really have nothing to fear.
> I'm not trying to tempt you,
>   that wouldn't be right;
> You shouldn't drink spirits at
>   this time of night —
> Have some Madeira, m'dear . . . .

Thus the advice of the naughty old gentleman in the Edwardian music hall song recalled so deliciously by Michael Flanders and Donald Swann — and there's no doubt that, whatever his dubious motives, their old roué knew a thing or two. For Madeira is not only the longest-living wine in the world but also among the most remarkable, able to match or surpass the roles of a wide range of other fortified wines.

Indeed, the name of the greatest Madeira wine, Malmsey, was familiar long, long before the music hall era. According to Shakespeare, picking up a legend from a century before his own time, the Duke of Clarence was removed as a rival for the throne by being drowned in a butt of Malmsey wine — murdered by order of his brother, the Duke of Gloucester, later King Richard III. Historically, that would have been about 1483.

Even if the story were true, which is doubtful, the Malmsey concerned was unlikely to have come from the island of Madeira, which was discovered only sixty-four years earlier. The wine which sealed Clarence's legendary fate, and which took its English name from the *Malvoisie* or Malvasia grape, would probably have been the Malmsey of Crete, in the Eastern Mediterranean (though the wine-growers of Cyprus claim that it was their cuttings which were taken by Portuguese explorers to establish the first vineyards in Madeira). Either way, once Madeira itself began exporting wines, they acquired such

77

popularity in Britain that, in the eighteenth century, they were often in even greater demand than sherry.

The hot little island of Madeira, only about one-third larger than the Isle of Man but with mountain peaks rising nearly 2000 metres (6000 feet) lies some 600 kilometres (400 miles) out into the Atlantic on the same latitude as the middle of Morocco. It was discovered about the year 1419 by a Portuguese explorer nicknamed 'Zarco the blue-eyed' — and it owes its great wines to a misguided decision which he took with the object of improving the island's agricultural prospects, but which turned out to be an act of vandalism.

When Zarco sailed in, Madeira was covered with dense forest. To clear some of the overgrowth and permit crops to be planted he ordered the trees to be set on fire. Unfortunately, the blaze got out of hand and took seven years to extinguish — by which time most of the thick forest had been reduced to a carpet of ash.

While it is true that this did considerably enrich the soil, the absence of trees also created problems of inadequate rainfall and irrigation. At the same time, Madeira's volcanic terrain, steep and rocky, provided just those tough, struggle-for-survival conditions on which the best vines seem to thrive — thereby opening the way for the island to produce really great wines.

These growths, today, comprise four main types, each named after the grapes from which they are made:

The aforementioned *Malmsey* — very sweet and luscious, with a strong and distinctive bouquet; usually dark brown in colour.

Bual (in Portuguese *Boal*) — sweet or medium-sweet, fragrant and with a velvet texture; golden brown in colour.

Verdelho — a half-way house, ranging between medium-sweet and medium-dry but usually tending more towards dry; lighter bodied than either of the above two wines; golden in colour.

Sercial — dry or very dry, light in colour, and particularly popular as an apéritif.

From their range of tastes, it is evident that Madeira wines, depending on their type, can be drunk before, during or after meals. In short, they combine the attributes of port and sherry, can offer an alternative to either — and may sometimes taste even better. However, although all are fortified wines, the method of producing Madeira has several marked differences from those used in making the others.

Madeira's vineyards lie in a vast series of terraces so steep that, often as not, the grapes have to be pressed on the spot — in press-houses scattered about the hillsides. Thereafter, the traditional method is for the 'must' to be poured into goatskin containers which are carried down the rough slopes, one per man, to the nearest road — the men easing their load with a strap across the forehead, as also used by workers in the port vineyards of the Douro.

From the pick-up point, lorries take the 'must' immediately to the lodges — the shippers' cellars in the towns — where it is fermented in wooden casks. The fermentation lasts about three weeks. Then comes the biggest difference of all — for Madeira is the only wine in the world to be given a 'Turkish bath' in the course of production. What happens is that the young wine is placed for up to six months in an *estufa*, or heated room, where the temperature is gradually raised to between 41° and 50° C (107° and 122° F), depending on the wine's quality, and is then, equally slowly, brought back to starting point.

Formerly, the wine was held in oaken barrels during this process. Nowadays, the job is usually carried out a little more quickly, in concrete vats (though barrels are still used for the finest wines).

The *estufa* process is derived from the ancient method of leaving casks out in the sun — a practice followed by Greek wine-growers to this day in making Mavrodaphne — and it doubtless explains the extraordinary longevity of Madeira wines. A good Madeira can easily live to be 100 years old, and there are still some in existence, in British cellars, which date back as far as the end of the eighteenth century!

Fortification of the Madeira wines is not administered with grape brandy, as used for port and sherry, but with a spirit distilled from the island's abundant sugar cane (one of those crops first planted by the intrepid Zarco). With the sweeter Madeiras of top quality, the spirit is added at an early stage, to prevent further fermentation and retain a fair amount of the wine's natural sugar before it turns into alcohol. With the drier types, most of the spirit is added after the *estufa* process. From then on, the wine is left to mature in cask for a year or more – though, here again, the finest growths may be kept in wood for a good deal longer. Once ready for bottling, Madeira may be produced as vintage, *solera* or blended. Vintage Madeira, from one given year, is now extremely rare – and to be prized above rubies if ever you get the chance to taste it.

In general, the best of the fine old Madeiras today are produced by the *solera* system, as used in making sherry. Accordingly, bear in mind that if you were to come across, say, a Malmsey *solera* 1821, this does not denote a specific vintage but gives the year in which the *solera* was laid down. It might have been bottled relatively recently, in fact. Nevertheless, you would be tasting a wine identical to the superb growth which was originally chosen to set the pattern, more than a century and a half ago.

Blended Madeiras, the final category, are the youngest and least expensive, comprising wines of different varieties and from different vineyards. Even these, however, will be anything from three to seven years old before they reach your wine merchant's shelves. Indeed, another outstanding trait of Madeiras of all types is that they show great improvement after several years in bottle – the longer the age in bottle, the better the flavour.

And one more

Although it does not strictly belong in this category, there is one dessert wine which shares some of the characteristics of fortified wines — albeit in a more natural way — and which has always been a bit of a Nimmo favourite. Schubert wrote a song about it; so did Noël Coward, in *Bitter Sweet*. Russia's Peter the Great thought so highly of it that he sent a battalion of the royal bodyguard to escort his supplies back to St Petersburg.

It's Tokay, the luscious Hungarian dessert wine which has been the subject of legends and almost unparalleled royal panegyrics for more than 300 years.

France's 'sun king', Louis XIV, called it 'the wine of kings and the king of wines'. He was doubtless well qualified to appreciate its beneficial effects, because he reigned for longer than any other monarch in recorded European history — some seventy-two years (which was six years or so more than Queen Victoria). Louis (1638-1715) was probably the first sovereign to bestow his personal favour on Tokay, initiating the fashion for it at other royal courts, for the special way to make the wine was discovered only about the time he came to the throne.

Despite the rapid renown acquired by Tokay, moreover, it owed its origins to a sheer fluke. The inhabitants of what is now Hungary have certainly been making wine since the occupying Roman legionaries were ordered to extend the local vineyards, by planting cuttings imported from their own country, in the third century A.D. Subsequently, cultivation was encouraged in turn by Attila the Hun, the invading Magyars from Asia, and then, after the country turned Christian, by the monasteries established under Stephen 1, Hungary's greatest king.

From 1526 onwards, however, Hungary was dominated by Turkish invaders and wine production was officially discouraged. For about two centuries, the country was ravaged by local wars — first, during the 160 years before the Moslem Turks were finally driven out by Habsburg troops, and then as the Hungarians rose in revolt against the Austrians.

It was during the seventeenth century that the steward of a royal vineyard in Hungary took the chance decision that gave birth to Tokay. Warned that fighting was imminent in the area, he ordered the vintage to be held up until the warring troops had gone. When the danger had passed, the secret of making superb sweet wines by deliberately gathering the grapes late, a secret lost since Roman times, had been accidentally rediscovered. . . .

That late-picking or *spälese* technique, as now associated with the greatest German wines, has been used in making Tokay ever since. Traditionally, the Tokay vintage does not begin until 28 October and lasts up to the end of November — anything from four to seven weeks later than the wine harvest in most other European countries. The technique is made possible by the presence of *pourriture noble*, the 'noble rot', the same grape fungus responsible for France's most outstanding sweet white wines (and notably the finest vintages of Sauternes, queen of them all).

Another happy accident due to the succession of wars on Hungarian soil was the discovery of the ideal cellar conditions for maturing Tokay. To hide it from the marauding soldiers, the growers stored the wine in low stone holes, often less than 2 metres (6 feet) deep, cut into the volcanic rock of the hillsides. Not only were the entrances to these makeshift cellars very difficult for invaders to detect, but it turned out that the black fungoid growth on the walls and the very cool temperatures inside (not more than 7° C (45° F) produced just the right conditions for the exceptionally slow fermentation essential for Tokay.

Today, production of the wine is restricted to twenty-five villages in a once-volcanic mountain district north-east of Budapest, near Hungary's border with Czechoslovakia. (Sweet white wines using the name Tokay are also made in two or three other countries, but these are in no way comparable with the real thing).

Altogether, three grape varieties are used in making the genuine article. Principal of these is the Furmint, a corruption of the French word *froment* (wheat); this is a dull yellow grape which was originally brought into the country in the thirteenth century by settlers from what is now the French-speaking area of Belgium. The other two varieties are Muscat grapes and a Hungarian type, the Harslevelu (linden-leaf).

In making the best-known type of Tokay, described as Tokay Aszu, the extra-sweet grapes shrivelled by the 'noble rot' are kept separate from the other, normally ripened grapes and are pressed in 30-litre (7-gallon) hods called *puttonyos*. Their fermenting juice (or 'must') is then added to the 'must' of the ordinary grapes. The more *puttonyos* that are added, the richer and sweeter is the eventual wine (and the more expensive, of course). The actual number will be shown on the bottle label, the word quite often being abbreviated to *putts*. Most Tokay Aszu is made with three, four or five puttonyos. Very occasionally, the growers may also produce some with six, but only in exceptionally great years.

This unique method has much the same purpose as the fortifying of other dessert wines like port and Madeira with brandy or wine spirit — that is, to prevent the fermentation from getting out of hand. It preserves the sweetness by ensuring that the natural sugar in the 'must' is not fermented right out. With Tokay, however, the essential difference is that, instead of arresting the fermentation with pure alcohol, the entire emphasis is on natural processes. These entail ceaseless care and control, particularly of temperature; a 'must' of such richness gives rise to technical problems which need the greatest skill to overcome.

Once the long and difficult fermentation is over, the wine is left to mature in cask, untouched, for a further four to eight years. The bungs are left out of the casks, which are not topped up, and the consequent contact with the air is said to give the wine a 'taste of bread'. The process gives Tokay exceptional keeping powers, making it almost as long-lived as Madeira. Bottles remaining in good condition for more than 200 years have been recorded. It is also unusual in that, even after a bottle has been opened, the wine will not deteriorate for many months.

All Tokay is bottled on the spot — it has to be, by law — and the wine is always shipped in distinctively-shaped half-litre bottles. Each bottle is numbered and shows the vintage on the label.

What with the length and complexity of production, the relatively limited quantity available and the extra transport costs of shipping in bottle, Tokay Aszu tends to be on the expensive side — though, in my view, far less so than one might have expected for such a masterpiece.

At a somewhat lower price level is another type — Tokay Szamorodni, which can be sweet or dry. (The word *szamorodni*, of Polish origin, means 'born of itself'.) The wine comes from the same vineyards as Tokay Aszu, but the difference is that both the 'noble rot' and ordinary grapes are pressed and fermented together.

The dry version, well cooled but not iced, is mostly drunk as an apéritif or with shellfish. The sweet version, drunk at room temperature, is a very pleasant dessert wine.

One last type which should be mentioned is the now extremely rare Tokay Essence. This is made solely from 'noble rot' grapes, placed in a special hod with a sieve at the bottom. The grapes are not pressed, but simply under their own weight produce a syrup-like juice which drips slowly through the sieve. Since the yield per 14-kilo (30-lb) hod is a mere 1.5 litres (3 pints) or so, the juice is so costly that it has been described as 'liquid gold'. Not surprisingly, therefore, Tokay Essence is no longer made for consumption — in the exceptional years when there are enough 'noble rot' grapes to permit it to be produced, anyway. Nowadays, it is used only for enriching the fine Tokay Aszu wines.

It was probably Tokay Essence which gave rise to the whispers among Victorian gentlemen about the supposed aphrodisiac properties of Tokay. Whether or not there was ever any truth in the rumour — which is not borne out by current experience, alas! — one point about which there is no question is the restorative and therapeutic qualities of all Tokay wines. You need only recall old Louis XIV.

Despite their richness, they are less strong in alcohol than many ordinary table wines. But the natural production of these lovely golden wines makes them a concentration of goodness. One small glass is enough for a health-giving 'lift'.

When all is said and done, though, Noël Coward conveyed what counts most through his chorus in *Bitter Sweet*:

'Tokay, the golden sunshine of a summer's day.' . . . That sums it up perfectly.

AUSTRALIA

It is almost a century since Australian wines began reaching the London market in large commercial quantities. Previously, they had been shipped to England only in small, sporadic amounts, though they had won prizes from the Royal Society of Arts as far back as 1820. For it is getting on for two centuries since wine was first made in Australia — virtually from the initial colonization of the country.

That was in 1788, when a fleet of eleven naval and merchant ships, under Captain Arthur Phillip, R.N., sailed through the headlands enclosing one of the world's greatest natural harbours and established what was to become the present-day city of Sydney.

The mixed cargo brought by Captain Phillip, later Governor of the colony of New South Wales, included a collection of vine cuttings. Some were planted immediately near the edge of the harbour, but the climate was wrong for them and they were not a success. The site is now part of the Sydney Botanical Gardens!

Much more successful was a vineyard planted at Parramatta, twenty miles inland — successful to such an extent that, before long, Governor Phillip was able to report that vine-growing had excellent prospects in the new colony.

These were the origins of an industry which, today, has a capital value estimated at some £100 million. Some idea of its development can be gauged from the fact that, at the Australian Wine Centre in London's Soho, more than 100 varieties of fortified and table wines are available.

Two men have each been described as the 'father' of Australia's wine industry. One was Captain John MacArthur — also said to have been the 'father' of the Australian Merino sheep industry. After a quarrel with the then Governor, the notorious Captain Bligh, he returned to Britain for a while and, with his sons James and William, made an eighteen-month tour of Europe to collect vines and study wine-making techniques. On his return to Australia he made the first serious attempt to establish a commercial vineyard in the colony, planted in 1820, the business being continued and expanded by his sons.

But my own preference, if only because of his sheer Scottish 'neck', is for the second candidate for the title, James Busby. An Edinburgh-born Northumbrian, he came to Sydney in 1824, aged twenty-three, and took a post as teacher at an orphanage. His salary of £100 a year embraced two responsibilities: to educate the orphans and to tend the small vineyard attached to the school.

Rapidly convinced that wine-making had a great future in the territory, he returned to England in 1830—31 and for several months made a tour of Europe's main vine-growing regions, from Jerez northwards. On the way , he persuaded many of the vineyards to make him gifts of cuttings — from 570 different varieties of vine, in all.

Not only that, but he persuaded Britain's Colonial Secretary of the day, Lord Goderich, to allow the huge collection, totalling some 20,000 cuttings, to be carried at Government expense 'on any of the convict ships about to sail, in order to secure their early and safe arrival in the Colony'.

Once back himself, Busby started a vineyard in the Hunter Valley, about 100 miles north of Sydney, and established nurseries to determine which of the cuttings he had imported were most suitable in the new terrain.

It is probable that Busby's initiative, in obtaining the pick of European grape varieties at one go, avoided a very long period of experimentation for Australia's infant wine industry and enabled the growers to find the best vines for each district many years earlier than would normally have been possible.

To this day, too, wine devotees in Australia regard the Hunter Valley district in much the same light as the French look upon Burgundy's Côte de Nuits or Bordeaux's Haut-Médoc. Certainly, its red and white table wines, though comprising less than 5 % of Australia's total production, are among the best in the country — comparable, perhaps, with some of the finest Côtes du Rhone.

However, it is not really a good guide to compare Australia's wines with those of other countries. Conditions of soil and sunshine give them entirely distinctive characteristics and they deserve to be appreciated in their own right.

Following James Busby's sterling efforts, vineyards

spread quickly to other parts of New South Wales and southwards into Victoria. Then it was found that the Barossa Valley, in South Australia, was ideal for the vine — and from there developments continued to the point that, nowadays, this one State produces more than 65 % of Australia's wine. On the far side of the Continent, many vineyards have also been planted in the fertile Swan Valley, near Perth.

Refrigeration and other modern scientific aids have made it possible for the growers to exercise full control over the fermentation of the wine — one of the major problems, originally, of wine-making in a very hot climate. Because of the prevailing heat, though, the Australian industry still has one unique feature.

In a country where so many regions have extreme temperatures and very sparse rainfall, there are bound to be a good number of otherwise suitable areas which have insufficient rain for vine-growing purposes. Accordingly, the wine districts are divided into two main types: the so-called 'dry' or non-irrigated areas, with an average annual rainfall of 20–30 inches, adequate for the vines' needs; and the irrigated areas, where water has to be pumped into the vineyards at key periods — in September, when leaf and cane growth is taking place, and in December and January (Australia's high summer months), when the bunches of grapes are filling out and ripening.

The crop in the irrigated vineyards can be four to five times heavier than in the 'dry' areas, but the wines tend to be of a lighter character. In the non-irrigated districts, the smaller crop per acre is usually counter-balanced by greater variety in the tastes and bouquets of wines produced.

Just under half of Australia's total output goes to make brandy or wine spirit, used for fortifying wines of the port and sherry types. Between the wars — particularly after the 1927 Budget, in which the then Mr Winston Churchill sharply increased the tariff preference for Commonwealth dessert wines — these Australian fortified wines became extremely popular abroad, particularly in Britain.

Recently, however, there has been a huge increase in the output of table wines — up by well over 500 % in only ten years. Indeed, although the Australians have long been legendary as beer drinkers, their annual consumption of wine is now nearly fourteen bottles a head. Specialist wine bars have become extremely popular, particularly with young people, and large numbers of such wine-only bars have opened throughout Australia.

A century ago, nobody bothered much about the adoption of names like Burgundy or Sauternes to describe wines from other countries. Australian 'Burgundy', for instance, was exported in the once-familiar flagon-shaped bottles only to distinguish it from the French product — but shippers made no bones about calling it by the French name.

These days, however, more and more of Australia's dry, full-bodied red table wines are being labelled principally under the name of the grape used in making them — and terms like Australian claret and Australian Burgundy have virtually disappeared from the labels.

This applies equally to the white table wines. As an example, one of the best wines from the Barossa Valley — not surprisingly, since many German immigrants settled there — is a 'Barossa Riesling', made from the authentic Rhine Riesling grape variety, now successfully grown in this part of South Australia. Nearly all the white wines are dry, crisp and refreshing, with a pleasing colour and bouquet: they are generally drunk young.

Another excellent Australian product, reasonably priced, is sparkling wine — the best of it made by the champagne method. In fact, there are very few types of wine that Australia does not produce.

NEW ZEALAND

We tend to think of New Zealand for its wool, lamb, beef, butter and other dairy products. But *wine*? Yes, indeed, for wine was first made on a commercial scale in New Zealand more than a century ago and the original European vines were probably planted there as early as 1815, the year of the Battle of Waterloo.

The man credited with planting them was the Rev. Samuel Marsden, an Anglican who, as chief chaplain to the New South Wales government, was not only the first missionary to New Zealand and among the first to bring European methods of agriculture to the islands but was also, through his enthusiastic reports to the Church Missionary Society, partly responsible for the British Government's decision to assume sovereignty over the territory.

Twenty years later, Marsden's vines were still flourishing — tended by Maori workers — at his mission station at Kerikeri, near the tip of New Zealand's North Island. We know this for sure because the fact was noted by none other than Charles Darwin when he landed there in 1835 during his round-the-world voyage in H.M.S. *Beagle*.

Another prominent figure in the pioneer days was James Busby, one of the two accepted 'fathers' of the Australian wine industry (mentioned in the previous section), who brought wine cuttings with him to New Zealand when he was appointed as its first Resident British Agent in 1833.

Busby, in his fervent advocacy of the virtues of the grape, wanted every settler to have his own small vineyard, hoping that wine would become so plentiful that people would drink it instead of beer or spirits. It is a delicious reflection of Victorian morality that in later years, presumably because it was held that his aspiration would help to reduce drunkenness, he was elected president of the new colony's first Temperance Society.

Five years after Busby planted his own vineyard at Waitangi, not far from Marsden's mission, a further batch of European vines was shipped in by Marist missionaries who had arrived from France. The Fathers needed wine for Mass, and, having settled somewhat farther to the south-east, in the Hawke's Bay region, duly established a vineyard there. Hawke's Bay remains among the best of New Zealand's wine-growing areas to this day and the Mission Vineyards are the oldest under the same management . . . (The Fathers' winery, incidentally, is also the only one in the country which produces a sparkling wine made by the 'champagne method').

However, the first New Zealand wine made specifically for commercial sale was grown by two people of somewhat less august origins.

One was Charles Levet, a coppersmith from Ely, in Cambridgeshire, who arrived with his family in mid-century and taught himself wine-growing from scratch, by reading it up in a book. By 1863, he and his son William, then fourteen, had cleared seven acres of land near the windy Kaipara harbour, north of Auckland, and eventually they were shipping barrels of wine to Auckland for the country's first licensed wine shop and bar — permitted opening hours, 6.0 a.m. to 10.0 p.m. daily! Levet concentrated on fortified wines, notably port and sherry styles, matured in oak for a minimum of five years, and his individual customers included two successive Governors of New Zealand, Sir William Jervois and Lord Glasgow (who allowed his name and crest to be used on Levet's bottle labels).

The other commercial pioneer was a Spaniard, Jose Soler, who had grown vines in his native Tarragona before settling at Wanganui, on the southern coast of North Island, in 1865. In the interim, he had visited Victoria, in Australia, to assess the prospects, but decided that New Zealand was a better bet for wine-making.

Soler was unusual in that he insisted on maturing his

light wines for at least eight years, grew only classical European grape varieties (such as the Riesling for his white wines and the Shiraz for red), and achieved their alcoholic content by entirely natural means, rejecting the practice of adding sugar for the purpose.

He was clearly a man of sound judgement, on all counts, as witness the large number of awards he received at wine exhibitions abroad. That great wine man André Simon has recounted how, at the Christchurch exhibition in 1906, Soler submitted five wines and won gold medals for three of them. This brought complaints from some of the Australian exhibitors, who demanded a re-judging; to placate them, a judge of whom they approved was selected to give the entries a fresh assessment. And this new judge gave Soler *five* gold medals!

With such promising antecedents, it may seem surprising that New Zealand wines are still virtually unknown to the outside world. But there are several reasons — stemming, in the past, from a sad mixture of missed opportunities, governmental and commercial short-sightedness, and natural disasters. Happily, they *are* in the past and the next few years should tell a very different story.

At the end of the nineteenth century, many of the country's vineyards began to be wiped out by the phylloxera pest which had already nearly destroyed Europe's finest vineyards. The only remedy, as in Europe, was to graft their own stocks on to American native vines, resistant both to phylloxera and to the mildew *(oidium)* suffered in the damp conditions in the north of the country.

Unhappily, the local growers found that these American vines gave a much bigger yield, by themselves, than the classical varieties. Although they produce inferior wine, usually described as having a 'foxy' taste, the growers could make more money by using them alone, without the bother or expense of the grafting process. For

— at that time, anyway — the majority of New Zealand's wine drinkers were indiscriminating and just wanted alcohol, not finesse.

It was not only that the coarse red wines, fortified to make them stronger, had a ready domestic market. In the first decades of the twentieth century, the growers also laboured under the continual threat of a prohibition campaign; so they naturally favoured dual-purpose grapes, which could be sold for the table if the prohibition threat was fulfilled. (The better-class wine grape varieties, of course, are *not* suitable as table grapes.)

This, in turn, highlights a further problem for the industry — the apathy of officialdom. Preoccupied with the greater tasks of nursing the country's crucial sheep, cattle and dairy farming interests, the New Zealand Government and its Department of Agriculture failed to give the wine industry either the support or the control necessary for maintaining and improving its standards. As a result, the country's estimated total of 668 acres under vine in 1909 had dwindled by 1923 to a mere 179 acres.

It was not until 1935, when a new government came to power, that steps were taken to encourage the industry, with funds allotted to enable it to acquire modern equipment and the local growers given protection by the levying of higher duties on imported wines.

Spurred on by the greatly increased demand during World War II, the upshot was that the acreage under vine grew from 665 in 1938 to 1252 in 1965 and, by the early 1970s, to 4500 acres – producing more than five million gallons of wine annually.

By then, too, the proportion of classical grape varieties used, as compared with other varieties not suitable for fine wines, had revived to around 60 %. This was still far short of conditions in the latter part of the nineteenth century, when the use of European grapes was almost total; but at least the growers were now turning again, more and more, to the making of good table wines instead of the stronger dessert wines hitherto mainly in popular favour locally.

No visiting expert has ever doubted New Zealand's capacity to produce fine wines. Its mainland lies between latitudes 34° and 47°, which is ideal temperate zone for wine-making. The city of Auckland is on the same latitude as Gibraltar. However, allowing for the inevitable differences between a continental land mass and a country surrounded by ocean, it's fair to say that conditions of climate in the Hawke's Bay area, for instance, are much the same as those in Bordeaux and Burgundy.

Some fifty years ago, a report to the New Zealand Government noted that such grape varieties as the Cabernet Sauvignon and Pinot Noir bore much heavier crops in New Zealand than in Europe. In recent years, there have been moves to plant more of them in the hope that such grapes, perhaps blended with others, will eventually produce the country's greatest wines.

The trend, certainly, has been gathering ever-increasing momentum. Famous wine companies from other countries — for instance, Harvey's of Bristol, Gilbeys and big Australian names like Penfolds and Seppelts — are now interesting themselves in the New Zealand wine industry, and the swing to good wine grows apace. In the U.K. a small quantity of New Zealand wine is already being imported by Avery's of Bristol.

One last factor. At present, the country's annual consumption averages about ten bottles a head. With its population around the three million mark, therefore, even an output of five million gallons of wine a year is barely sufficient to meet domestic demand (especially since better stocks must be kept back and allowed time to mature).

However, as table wine production continues to grow, the point is at last being reached when there is the prospect of a reasonable surplus for export.

So I'm not being fanciful when I hazard a guess that, over the next decade, the best New Zealand white wines may become as familiar to wine drinkers in other countries as those of, say, Alsace or Provence. And as well accepted, too.

SOUTH AFRICA

One of the great mysteries that has fascinated European wine-growers for centuries is whether they have entirely recaptured the wine-making secrets of the early Romans. From all accounts, the best Roman wines were quite superb . . . but they vanished in the obscurity of the Dark Ages after Rome fell to the Barbarians, and it is thought that – like stained glass and other ancient skills – some of the original arts have yet to be rediscovered.

Well, that's as may be. But there's a 'lost secret' in the wine world much nearer our own day; in fact, almost within living memory. The wine concerned, called Constantia, had a big vogue in England from the end of the eighteenth century into the 1860s and was praised by such diverse characters as Napoleon, Jane Austen and the French poet Baudelaire.

'Old Constantia' was made in South Africa and first found its way to Europe in quantity after Britain took possession of the Cape from the Dutch. It is known to have been a very rich, smooth dessert wine (probably not unlike an extremely good Madeira). Subsequently, however, a series of troubles hit the local vineyards, spread over more than fifty years, and by then the secret had been lost. Although muscat-flavoured Constantia wines are again being made, they are not quite the same as before. Nobody has been able to re-create the original, supreme version.

In the late seventeenth century, Huguenot refugees, skilled in wine-growing traditions already centuries old, rapidly extended and improved the Cape's vineyards. Conditions, they found, were ideal – generous rainfall in winter, six months of uninterrupted but not too hot summer sun, and a virtual absence of rain during the critical period just before the harvest in the autumn.

Among the Huguenot settlements were Franschhoek (the first half of the name echoing its French assocation). Drakenstein and Stellenbosch; above all, they founded the town of Paarl, in a mountain valley thirty-six miles inland from Cape Town, which is now the headquarters of the South African wine industry.

To this day, despite the enormous expansion of the industry, virtually all of it remains within 150 miles of Cape Town. The vineyards cover two main districts — the Coastal Belt, centred on Paarl; and, beyond the first mountain range, the Little Karoo, centring on the towns of Worcester, Montagu and Robertson. Broadly speaking, the wines become heavier as they go inland. The finest, most delicate wines come from the Coastal Belt. The Little Karoo, higher in altitude, and with most of its vineyards needing to be irrigated, tends to produce fuller wines, particularly dessert wines and sweet South African sherry.

However, that is a generalization. The Cape makes wines of every kind: red, white and rosé table wines, port styles and South African sherry (the production of which is described in detail on pages 71-3), sparkling wines, brandies, even a number of liqueurs — including one unique to South Africa. This last, the mandarin-flavoured Van der Hum, was originally made by the early settlers in their own homes and is said to have been named after a Dutch sea captain who had a legendary fondness for it. . . .

Cape wines enjoyed their first big boom in Britain from the Napoleonic era onwards, when the British Government encouraged wine imports from other sources as part of their measures to 'dish' the French; by 1824, their annual exports had risen to a peak of one million gallons - - enormous, when you consider the much smaller populations of those days.

Subsequently, though, the industry began to suffer the consequences of the gradually improving relations between Britain and France; and in 1861, when the

Gladstone Government abolished the last of the tariff preferences which had enabled the Cape growers to compete with European countries, their export trade with Britain collapsed.

Having invested substantial capital to build up their production, the farmers were now faced with chronic surplus. Then, in the 1880s, they were hit by the phylloxera disease, which was also ravaging Europe's vineyards. Yet even this did not solve the problem of over-production, which, in the early 1900s, resulted in Cape wines selling for as little as a penny a bottle!

All these vicissitudes have a place in the present story because — much like the vine itself, which tends to produce better quality when it has to struggle in difficult rather than easy soil — the long series of troubles led directly to the huge success now enjoyed by the Cape wine industry.

Towards the end of World War I, the farmers realized that they could not hope to overcome the problems individually and therefore formed a co-operative which became responsible for control of both wine production and marketing. This body, the Co-operative Wine-growers' Association (usually known as the K.W.V., from the initials of its name in Afrikaans), originally had just over 1900 members. Today, there are some 5000 of them and the K.W.V. has played a predominant part in helping to secure a higher reputation and bigger share of international markets for Cape wines than ever before.

The organization lays down minimum wine prices, fixes quotas to prevent over-production, has built up stocks of matured, quality wines in its cellars at Paarl running into many millions of gallons — cellars which have earned an entry in the *Guinness Book of Records* as 'the largest in the world' — and has also established ultra-modern laboratories to carry out research and quality control.

Although a few large growers have remained outside

the organization — at least two of them produce some of the country's best table wines — the K.W.V. has a supervisory role to ensure that the highest standards are maintained. Wine sales by the independents are subject to its approval, and the K.W.V. itself sells nine-tenths of all the country's wine exports.

Yet it is not a government body, the directors are still themselves wine farmers, elected to the Board by their fellow growers in the various wine-producing areas.

All of which helps to explain why Cape wines have been earning an increasing reputation, world-wide, for their sound quality and reliability.

Grape varieties by the Cape growers include such traditional French types as Cabernet Sauvignon, Pinot Noir, Shiraz, Gamay, Hermitage and Clairette Blanche, as well as the red and white Muscat grape for dessert wines, together with the Spanish Palomino and Portuguese grapes from the Douro valley. However, they also make some South African sherries and dry white wines from a grape called the Steen, a variety found nowhere else in the world. The Steen developed naturally from the vines planted by the first settlers more than 300 years ago, and this provides a clue to the future prospects of the Cape wine industry. For, more and more, the local growers are seeking to put a truly individual stamp on their products and to create wines which, like Old Constantia in its day, will be ranked with the best European growths.

The Wine Drinker's Etiquette

STORING AND SERVING WINE

Once you have found out from experience which wines you particularly like, it's well worth buying in a small stock of them at home. That isn't self-indulgence nor extravagance, but merely sound sense. Having your own 'cellar' enables you to take advantage of occasional wine bargains you may spot when out shopping, even if you don't want to drink them just then; it also ensures that you always have a reasonable bottle on hand if you have guests to dinner without much warning.

Storing wine so that is stays in good nick is much easier than many people fear. The only essentials are that it should be kept somewhere fairly dark, out of the draught, and not subject to sudden changes of temperature, nor vibration, and also that the bottles should be laid flat (to prevent the cork shrinking and letting in air, which could cause the wine to deteriorate).

Provided you can meet these conditions, it doesn't matter where in the home you keep it. A cellar is ideal, naturally, but few people have cellars nowadays — at least, not in modern houses or flats. Failing that, a cupboard under the stairs will also serve perfectly well, assuming it is not disturbed too frequently. For flat-dwellers, a dark corner at the back of the airing cupboard could be a reasonable solution. It might be a trifle too warm, though; in which case, you'd do better to keep white wines, anyway, on the floor of the pantry (or equivalent).

As for laying the wine flat, I've seen some excellent self-assembly wine racks, holding a dozen bottles, for only about £3. However, there's no need to go to the expense if you don't want to. As a makeshift, an empty wooden wine crate, laid on its side, is quite adequate for the job.

Now, what about serving the stuff? First, the corkscrew. The best kind to use in my view is a plain one with a broad, longish spiral. I find that those corkscrews with a narrow, gimlet-like spiral tend to pull out of old or inferior corks.

Next, immediately you've opened the bottle, always wipe its mouth with a clean cloth before pouring any wine from it. Even if you can't see them, tiny bits of muck are bound to have stuck to it. They are only fragments of cork and dust, and probably quite harmless, but get rid of them.

Before you get down to the drinking, bear in mind that it isn't chi-chi but a matter of plain fact that all wines taste better if served at their right temperatures. For all white wines and most rosé, that means cool or chilled (though not ice-cold); for red wines, it means 'room temperature', which is about 20° C (68° F).

Both are quite easy to achieve. With white wine, get out the bottles about half an hour to an hour before drinking and put them in an ice-bucket or in the main compartment of your fridge (*never* the freezer). Or, in cold weather, simply put them outside the back door for the same period. When on country trips or picnics, the best expedient is to wrap the bottle in a cold wet cloth, or even damp newspaper. And if you happen to be having a picnic beside a river or lake, of course, you can always tie a piece of string round the neck and dunk the bottle in the water for half an hour or so.

For red wines, it may seem that, short of actually tasting them, room temperature could be hard to judge precisely. In fact, though, the simplest way is to put the back of your hand on the bottle; if the glass has no obvious feeling of coldness, it'll be about right. But please, please, *never* try to speed up the process by heating a bottle of red wine near a fire or running hot water over it — that is, not unless you really like your wine 'cooked'. Far better to let it get there naturally by drawing the cork an hour before the meal and leaving the bottle on the table.

The only exceptions to the 'room temperature' serving of red wines are a few young light reds like Beaujolais and the Italian Valpolicella and Bardolino, which *can* be drunk cool — and are deliciously refreshing that way.

As for how much wine to allow per person, when entertaining guests, you can reckon on getting up to six decent glasses from a standard-size bottle of wine (or up to eight glasses from a 1-litre size). Assuming each person drinks two glasses, therefore, one bottle is about right for three people –but for only two if they're rather more thirsty types!

What amount to pour into the glass each time? In principal, it should be filled to not more than two-thirds of the way up, never to the brim. How else can you get your nose in to sniff that beautiful smell?

If there is a glassful or two left in the bottle after the meal, you can certainly put the cork back and store it for a while. Preferably, though, *not* for more than two to three days before finishing it. Once a table wine has been exposed to the air, that's about the longest it will last before starting to go off.

Two last suggestions

When re-sealing a bottle, I always reverse the cork, i.e. so that the end which was originally inside the neck now goes uppermost.

Like full bottles, half-full ones should also be kept in conditions as undisturbed as possible. For white wines, find some fairly cool place but don't put them back into the fridge — at least, not until half an hour or so before you plan to finish off the bottle. Not to worry if you have no opportunity to drink the odd glass or two left in the bottle within the two to three days I have recommended, and please don't just ditch it. You can always keep it to use for cooking, indefinitely.

THROUGH A GLASS LIGHTLY

A great French gastronome named Eugene Plumon — the sort of man who really could identify almost any wine you offered him — was completely unpretentious. And he once said: 'I see nothing wrong in drinking wine from a toothmug, if that's all you happen to have handy.'

Without taking him too literally, I've often felt that more nonsense is talked about the supposedly 'correct' glasses for this or that wine than about almost any other aspect of wine in general. For the fact is that there are just two standard types of wine-glass which are perfectly O.K. for all normal purposes.

As a broad guideline, it is preferable that your wine glasses should be fairly thin, uncoloured, uncut, reasonably (but not excessively) generous in size, and if possible with at least a small stem. And there is no need to spend a fortune on them. Many stores sell glasses fully adequate for everyday requirements, which cost little more than 30p each. These are standard glasses and, of course, you will also find more expensive kinds, in different shapes and sizes. Why so many variations? Leaving aside the purely decorative aspect, there *is* usually a valid explanation for them. For instance, Germany's hocks and Moselles are served, habitually, in long-stemmed glasses because these wines are always drunk chilled, so it makes sense to have a glass which can be held where the warmth of your hand doesn't get through to the wine. Similarly, the dimensions of some types — liqueur glasses, for example — may be dictated simply by what is the appropriate measure for the wine concerned.

At a pinch, though, even these special functions can be met quite satisfactorily by the two standard types of wineglass I mentioned earlier — the 'tulip' and the 'ballon'. The 'tulip' is like a half-opened tulip on a medium-tall stem; the 'ballon' is like the bottom half of a small balloon or globe. Both styles have rims which curve in slightly, helping to retain the bouquet or aroma of the wine. They'll even serve to retain the bubbles of sparkling wine, if that's what you happen to be drinking.

Besides the 'tulip', another type of glass preferred by the *cognoscenti* for drinking champagne is the *flûte* — the French word for a tall, narrow glass, like a thin, inverted cone, without a stem. On that score, the one type of glass to be avoided at all costs is the saucer-shaped monstrosity often used for champagne at weddings. Its open shape loses the bubbles far too quickly. In fact, this kind of glass is thought to have been invented by caterers during the Victorian era merely as an aid to speeding up consumption!

TASTING IT OUT

Great Chinese chefs say that good food should appeal to all five senses: it should be attractive to look at, a pleasure to smell, feel good in the mouth, produce a proper sound when masticated and, naturally, appeal to the taste.

Except, perhaps, for the sound effects, the same characteristics apply when you're sampling a wine. (And even then, many professional tasters do indeed make quite a noise, through a trick they have of leaving a little wine in the front part of the mouth and drawing in air sharply over it, to get the full savour more quickly. It really works — try it yourself.)

Although the customary term is wine 'tasting', I've long felt that *testing* would be a more accurate word; and the first test, in my view, should always be the colour. Is it an aesthetically pleasing colour, bright and clear? No clouding or suspended matter?

The best way to make sure is to look at the glass of wine against a light source — the window, say, or a white table cloth. For the same reason, the wine glass itself, as explained in the previous section, should be plain, uncut, untinted, and preferably with a small stem so that the warmth of your hand does not get through to the wine.

Next, the bouquet or aroma, which may remind you of specific fruits like raspberries or strawberries, of honey, herbs, or flowers like violets. Not every wine has a strong bouquet, particularly those from hot climes, but all should be at least faintly evocative of *something* pleasant. The fact that the 'nose' is an alternative word sometimes used for the bouquet is certainly appropriate. If you watch professional wine buyers at work, you'll see that they really do stick their noses deep inside the glass.

Many years ago, I attended a tasting session prior to an auction sale of rare ports and brandies; and I was fascinated to note that the buyers identified each one by its 'nose' alone. Not once did any of them refer to the catalogue for confirmation; they did so only to jot down, against each lot number, the figure they were prepared to bid for it.

The next test is that of feel and taste. How a wine feels good in the mouth varies greatly. Some have such a full effect that you almost find yourself 'chomping' them. Others leave a delightful after-taste lingering behind them. Whatever its specific form, the sensation speaks for itself. Only you can tell.

Finally, the taste. While drinking the stuff is the bit we all look forward to, it could also be regarded, paradoxically, as the least important of the tests. Because, by the time you get there, it should merely serve to confirm what all your previous testing has already told you about the wine.

On the surface, there is an inevitable vagueness about describing these four steps in wine tasting. It's a matter of language. After all, how could you describe a colour to someone who has never seen it? It is virtually impossible, of course. The same would appear to apply when trying to pass on, verbally or in writing, the varying sensations experienced in appraising a wine. Yet the odd thing is that professional wine tasters, however vague and esoteric their jargon may seem, are anything but imprecise in their judgements. If a group of them were asked to assess an unidentified wine by giving it marks out of 100, say, they would rarely differ by more than four or five marks, at the most. That level of near-unanimity – far more exact than you would ever find among music or art critics, for instance – is neither necessary nor even desirable, perhaps, for us ordinary mortals when trying out wines with friends or family. For you and me, the customers, there's only one opinion-standard that matters: 'if I like it, it's good'. And this, indeed, should always be our attitude to wine in general, irrespective of anyone else's views.

Even so, it is still worth following the tasting sequence practised by the professionals – that is, taking each of a wine's different characteristics in turn – to help one reach a personal verdict with more confidence.

WHAT GOES WITH WHAT

When you've found a wine that you like more than most, there is nothing to stop you drinking it with every course of a meal, if you wish. The old-fashioned wine snobs, insisting dogmatically that only this or that wine was the 'correct' accompaniment to this or that food, overlooked one all-important fact: in the real everyday world, individual palates differ and wine is entirely a matter of personal taste.

For instance, the dogma says that you should only drink

'I'm sorry, sir, but the head waiter won't allow me to serve
Burgundy with a prawn cocktail.'

white wine with fish. Yet the fact is that a good few people regularly drink light red wine with it.

It is true that red wine may taste rather metallic if the fish is seasoned with vinegar or other sharp sauces. Another reaction shared by the majority of people (though not everyone) is that red wines seem somewhat bitter with desserts or other sweet foods. Similarly, sweet wines tend to become a bit cloying when drunk with savoury dishes.

These general reactions show why certain broad tendencies about 'what with what' have become established over the years. But they *are* only tendencies, not inflexible rules. Just treat them as advice — but stick with what you personally happen to prefer; it doesn't matter a jot if your palate doesn't accord with majority opinion, and it's certainly no reflection on your standards of taste!

At the same time, while recognizing that many of the old 'rules' were pretty irrelevant, it's worth reading what people say in wine articles (and in books, as well, I'm glad to say!) — particularly if it helps you to get more enjoyment from the subject *and* more value for money. You can always ignore wine advice, which when you try it out, strikes you in practice as snobby and unnecessary.

That being said, there is no doubt that many people are still unsure about which combinations of food and wine go best together, particularly if they are entertaining guests who may not share their own preferences. So, on the strict understanding that it is intended only for guidance, not as a list of rules, here is an outline of what prevailing experience *suggests* as the combinations of food and wine that go best together:

Soup, hors d'oeuvres
Dry or medium-dry sherry, or you might try a dry Madeira . . . it costs little more than sherry and makes an unusual change, whether with food or as an apéritif by itself.

Fish, shellfish, cold chicken and the like

Dry or medium-dry light white wines. As examples: Yugoslav Laski Riesling; a cool dry Muscadet from France's Loire region; or a Soave from Italy — the last-named often being sold nowadays in economic large-size bottles.

Straightforward meats: lamb, beef, roast chicken

Lighter to medium-bodied red wines. I'd recommend claret, or Beaujolais; alternatively, try Valpolicella or Bardolino, from Italy.

Stronger meats: duck, goose, game, stews

Fuller-bodied red wines. For instance: Burgundy, or Côtes du Rhône, from France; Bull's Blood from Hungary; or Rioja and Valdepenas from Spain.

Dessert (sweets, ices, fruit, etc.)

Sweet white wines (still or sparkling). Among those which spring to mind are Sauternes or Barsac from France; Asti Spumante from Italy; Sekt from Germany; and, of course, champagne, which can happily be drunk right through the meal, in fact, if you're splashing out.

Cheese, nuts

Port, sweet Madeira, sweet sherry. You can also finish off your red wine with the cheese — they go excellently together. Indeed, most French people have their cheese before the dessert, for that reason.

There are two other types of food I ought to mention which have become increasingly popular in the last twenty years — Chinese and Indian. Not only are the restaurants serving them still very reasonable in price but they are also very handy as take-away meals. Either way, lots of people think one should only drink tea with Chinese food and beer or lager with hot Indian curries, to help cool the mouth. In fact, though, well-chosen wines are not only delicious with both types of food but even help to enhance them.

With Chinese food, some people drink dry rosé wines, like Anjou and Tavel. Light, dry, white wines are equally suitable. Besides those I've already suggested with fish and cold chicken, you might try a German Liebfraumilch or a Moselle like Bernkasteler or Piesporter, though personally I much prefer China tea with Chinese food.

To offset hot curries, appropriate choices would be medium white wines, such as Entre-deux-mers or Niersteiner; alternatively, full-bodied dry red table wines – St Emilion or Chianti, say — will help to bring out the flavour, while also being refreshing.

Finally, if you're giving a slap-up dinner with a number of different wines, here are a few rules-of-thumb about the order of precedence: a dry wine should be drunk before a sweet one, a younger before an older, a white before a red. However, a dry red wine should go before a sweet white, irrespective of their ages: the question of age precedence applies only to reds and whites separately, not combined. It would be quite in order to serve an older white wine before a young red. Ideally, though, the succession of wines during a meal should if possible build up to a peak of greatness, i.e. your best wine with the best main course.

The wines I have cited above are merely a very few of the many which would go just as well with each category. The only real way to decide which go best is to experiment for yourself. Happily for us all, it is — to coin a phrase — fun finding out.

THE GREAT OUTDOORS

Going on a picnic? Perhaps you've been planning it for quite a while and the grub has all been prepared and packed up carefully in a handsome wicker basket the

'I don't know whether or not jogging is doing Sir Humphrey any good but it's killing his butler.'

night before. Or maybe there's suddenly a hot day and, on the spur of the moment, you stop off to buy some bread, pâté, fruit and cheese before whisking off to the sea or the countryside.

Either way, a bottle or two of wine will add a lot to the pleasure of the day. Whether you're just taking sandwiches and hard-boiled eggs or something more special like a cooked chicken (which has the advantage of being easy to cut and uncomplicated to eat), the chances are that the weather will lend itself to light white wines, rosés or even sparkling wine.

Despite the travelling, it's not difficult to keep them cool. Put the bottle in your fridge for an hour or so before you leave, then wrap it in a damp cloth (or wet newspaper) and lay it in the boot of your car, placed so that it doesn't roll about, until you're ready to drink it. If you picnic near a lake or river, as I suggested in an earlier chapter, tie a piece of string to the bottle and cool it in the water for half an hour before the meal. Or better still, buy a polystyrene insulating box.

It is always worth buying some cheap glasses or tumblers for picnic use — they needn't cost more than a few pence each. There is something about drinking wine from plastic beakers which reduces it to the teeth-cleaning level. You can't see the colour of the wine properly; and even if you're not actually tasting the plastic, you often feel that you are. . . .

Oh, yes, and there's one other little item whose absence, however lovely the weather, is positively guaranteed to ruin the day: DON'T FORGET THE CORKSCREW!

Barbecues
Just as you can take cooked meats, fresh fruit and tasty cheeses which make picnics much more interesting than routine sandwiches, so it is possible to get far more variety into an open-air barbecue than the traditional chops, steaks or sausages. Fish, poultry, corn-on-the-cob and

111

potatoes in their jackets are only a few of the many other foods you can cook on a barbecue quite easily. (If you're short of flat grid space, wrap the potatoes in foil and put them straight on to the charcoal.) The only essential precaution is to light the fire beforehand, not just at the time you want your meal. Cooking can begin only when the charcoal is red hot, which usually takes about half an hour.

To prevent the fire from flaring, it is advisable to cut off all the fat from the meat before cooking it. But you can make up for that by brushing the meat with a sauce produced from 85 grams (3 ounces) of melted butter and half a glass of white wine.

You should have no problems with the wines to crown the feast — whether full red to go with thick steaks and chops, or whites, rosés or sparkling wines with lighter foods. You need merely get them ready as usual in the house and then ask someone to bring them out into the garden a couple of minutes before you start serving up the meal. Large-size bottles of the many inexpensive table wines are ideal for this type of party.

A word of warning, though — always try to have appreciably more wine glasses than the number of guests. People tend to put them down and forget about them; or they may want to switch to another type of wine. If there aren't enough spare glasses, you'll be spending much of your party in the kitchen washing up!

WINE IN THE RESTAURANT

Ordering wine in a restaurant puts many people in a flutter, particularly when faced with a very long wine list. The topic arose the other day while I was chatting with a member of the Guild of Sommeliers, the top wine waiters in the English-speaking countries, and he had some good advice to offer.

Firstly, however swish the restaurant, the basic approach to wine is no different from that in your own home: you start by deciding what you're going to eat and *then* choose what to drink with it. If you're still not sure, ask the wine waiter's advice. Tell him what dishes you'll be eating (and, if necessary, the maximum price you're prepared to pay for your wine).

Secondly, don't try to bluff your way through. All too often, it results in a choice of wine unsuitable for the food concerned. The bluffers betray themselves, my sommelier friend revealed, because almost invariably (when the wine

'Pierre recommends the Mouton Rothschild '70 with everything. It's the only wine in the cellar he doesn't drink himself.'

list is fairly small) they simply order the second most expensive one on the list. . . . And he bemoaned the number who fail to consult him when he's standing by, longing to be helpful — which does *not* mean he recommends only the dearest bottles. As he observed: 'We want our customers to come back — not to frighten them away!'

If your wine waiter wears the Guild of Sommeliers' silver badge, you'll know that he is specially trained and attends lectures and wine-tastings in his spare time. In short, you can rely on him.

When in doubt, don't regard wine in carafe as beneath you. Many restaurants take care to choose decent quality carafe wines, offering a trio of white, red and rosé, and they're nearly always good value for money. Alternatively, most restaurants these days will also sell you wine by the glass, if you prefer.

BUYING WINE AT AUCTION

Newspaper stories about the main wine auctions inevitably focus on the freak prices paid by collectors for exceptional rarities, such as £1550 paid not long ago for a jeroboam (equal to six bottles) of Château Mouton Rothschild 1929 — which worked out at just over £43 a glass!

However, it is still relatively easy to find good buys at wine auctions. What is more, this doesn't apply only to obscure country-house sales, reputedly the source of most of the fantastic bargains one hears about. Even at the big city auctions, not all the wine sold is of specially high quality or of interest to collectors.

In recent years, far more generally than before, the salerooms have become an accepted way of buying and selling wine (even though leading auctioneers have been holding periodic wine sales, in fact, since the eighteenth century).

Among the advantages of acquiring wine in this day is that you don't necessarily have to buy it 'blind'. Often as not, a tasting is held the day before the sale, or sometimes on the actual morning of the auction so that would-be purchasers can try the wine before making their bids (at auctions with a fair amount of wine on offer, anyway). It is not likely to apply, of course, if there are just a few odd lots.

Probably the best way to land yourself a bargain — even if professionals are in the field, is to form a syndicate or buying group with three or four friends or business associates. Your syndicate will then be able to bid for larger lots, which frequently sell at lower price levels, per bottle, than small ones do.

The size of lots differs a great deal. Some salerooms offer lots of one or two dozen bottles, but most lots offered are of three, four or five cases. Occasionally, the lots may comprise as many as fifteen, twenty or twenty-five cases, which can get jolly expensive overall. For an important point to bear in mind is that, except for very small batches of variegated bottles, bidding is always conducted at the rate per case (i.e. a dozen bottles, six magnums or twenty-four half-bottles). So, if you were to buy a lot of three cases for a hammer price of £16, say, the actual purchase price would be £48. Still, as I've suggested, that would be no great strain on the pocket if you were splitting it with friends afterwards.

Buying wine at auction is not a complicated affair, and most auction houses produce leaflets setting out details of their sales and saleroom procedure. They even bid on behalf of buyers who are unable to attend the sale (you merely have to tell them, in advance, the maximum you're prepared to pay).

If, instead of being a purchaser, you've some wine that you'd like to dispose of, selling it at auction is also reasonably straightforward. While each auction house has its own procedures, these — as with buying — do not vary much from one house to another. Usually, vendors are required to deliver the wine to a central point before the sale, generally the saleroom itself or a central store, but distribution of the wine to its new owners is arranged by the auctioneers after the sale.

To the wine trade, the salerooms provide a comprehensive service. Many wine merchants keep an eye on auction prices and use the results as a basis for their wholesale/retail price lists. Salerooms are also a valuable outlet for the trade. Some wine merchants periodically 'try the market' for a certain wine or a certain vintage, just to see what prices are like in an open market situation. Auctions also provide the trade with a relatively rapid outlet for excess stocks and are particularly handy if a company needs to raise some cash fairly quickly for reinvestment.

Whether trade or private customer, the fundamental point to bear in mind is that the salerooms are a market place. That certain wines are sometimes cheaper or more expensive than others has very little to do with fashion or snobbery. To a great extent, auction prices are governed simply by the laws of supply and demand.

All that counts is your own opinion. If you spot a wine that you like and decide to make a bid, it doesn't matter that few other people at the sale seem interested in it and there's little bidding against you. On the contrary, you're lucky. For *you*, that's a bargain!

How Not To
Be a Wine Snob

What is a wine snob? For a start, he's almost certainly a man. (I can recall only two women who came anywhere near qualifying for such an accusation.) He's a man 'who uses a knowledge of wine, often imperfect, to impress others with a sense of his superiority.' That's the definition given in a new edition of the late Raymond Postgate's *Plain Man's Guide to Wine*, revised by John Arlott. The wine snob, it adds, will imply that ignorance of certain elaborate conventions is socially disastrous, by telling anecdotes of others who made errors which he was able to correct.

He insists that you should know the good, moderate and bad years since 1900 for half-a-dozen or so various categories of wine. (It doesn't seem to strike him that this would involve memorizing more than 1300 different verdicts – nor that, within any given region, one vineyard may sometimes have had a poor vintage in a year when its neighbours did well, and vice-versa.)

The snob is finicky, too, about precisely which kind of glass should be used for each type of wine and exactly what foods are 'right' for it. In short, he's the kind of man to drive a newcomer to wine-drinking straight back to beer!

Not one of the genuine experts I've met in the wine business, here or abroad, is guilty of such pretentiousness. They have a deep love and respect for the subject, certainly, but otherwise a completely matter-of-fact, undogmatic approach. Indeed, all these specialists would

117

'Damn male chauvinist . . .!'

agree with the anti-snob advice given in Postgate's book: 'Drink what you like. Do what you wish. Don't pretend.'

The nonsense they deplore was illustrated by an article in a leading daily newspaper, written by a restaurateur and entitled, 'What anyone dining out should know before he orders the wine'. For concentrated balderdash, it proved a classic. Among its choicer idiocies was: 'Don't be afraid to ask for your Beaujolais to be chilled in an ice-bucket for ten minutes, even if the wine waiter thinks you're a nut. *Everyone in Beaujolais and Lyon does so.*' (His italics).

Quite apart from the silly snobbism of spelling Lyon in its French style for an English-speaking audience, his comment just isn't true. For *young* Beaujolais, yes — delicious when cool. But there are more mature Beaujolais wines which the locals would deem it a crime to quaff that way, as they would the better-class Beaujolais growths such as Morgon, Brouilly, Moulin-à-Vent and Chiroubles.

Here are two more assertions by the same worthy: 'Almost any red wine improves by decanting it,' and 'Avoid drinking carafe wines.'

Obviously, this 'advice' could be valid on some occasions, but neither point should be regarded as a blanket rule. On the contrary, decanters are unnecessary except for crusted port and other wines with sediment; and most restaurants usually take pains to offer carafe wines of good value.

I ought to add, perhaps, that one shouldn't over-compensate by accepting the view of the 'nothing to it' folk who say the only thing to know about wine is how to open the bottle. People interested in cooking, angling or gardening take it as a matter of course to read articles and books on the subject. So there are good grounds for doing likewise with wine, to some extent. Clearly, though, it's as well to be discriminating about *whom* you read. . . .

This was also borne out by one of those long and

weighty appraisals of a hundred or so plonks on the market, published in a Sunday paper magazine. The lofty dismissals of nearly everything they tasted, by the alleged experts who conducted the survey, made me positively angry. Not because I had a particular axe to grind for any of the wines they condemned but because I felt they were misleading their readers.

I admit frankly that I've encountered two or three cheap blended wines, sold under resounding brand names, which I hope never to have to sample again. Too rough, too sweet, conducive of indigestion . . . the cause doesn't greatly matter, for individual palates differ. What *does* matter is that even the best wines will taste awful if they're not looked after properly. All too often, for instance, small local shops (as distinct from specialist wine merchants) are guilty of keeping bottles in the window for, maybe, weeks on end, with the result that eventually the sun causes them to become browner in colour and sometimes quite vinegary. It is such shopkeepers who should be condemned and not necessarily the wines themselves, which might have been reasonably drinkable if they'd been kept correctly.

So the lesson is plain. When buying wine, you'll know that shops which keep bottles protected from excessive light and sharp changes of temperature have, at least, a decent respect for their products. If a store doesn't observe such simple precautions, don't give it your custom. After all, to expect certain minimum standards, as long as they are within reason, isn't the same thing as being snobbish!

WINE TERMS

It is possible to be knowledgeable about wine without becoming a wine snob and, over the years, I've had a lot of fun trying to master some of the official 'wine terms'. Here's Nimmo's Guide to the terms you might actually come across and might even find it useful to understand.

Age is often thought to be desirable in a wine – but it ain't necessarily so. While a good number of wines do improve with age (particularly the best clarets and red Burgundies), there are many others which go over the top if left for very long and they should be drunk at the latest within three to five years of their being made. Among these are all rosés, most of the lighter Italian wines, Beaujolais, dry Graves and most dry Loire wines.

Appellation Contrôlée (likewise Appellation d'Origine Contrôlée), sometimes abbreviated to A.C. or A.O.C., is a mark of status for French wines, legally defined by French government decree. It is not a guarantee of high quality, as such, but it does confirm that the wine: comes from the particular area, town or individual vineyard that the label says it does; is produced only from the grape varieties specificed for that wine and in quantities which do not exceed the maximum yield per acre laid down for it; and has been produced in accordance with local custom and the traditional practice of the district concerned.

So, although A.C. doesn't specifically promise top quality, you can take it that wines granted an Appellation are certainly *likely* to be above average. Indeed, all France's greatest wines belong to this category.

Balance is one of the most complimentary terms you can apply to a wine. It means that the wine has all the qualities it should have and that these qualities are present in the correct proportions. In a balanced wine, no single characteristic will ever dominate the others – there will be a perfect harmony of bouquet, flavour, body, aroma and aftertaste.

Big, applied to wine, says that it has more than the usual share of alcohol, body and flavour – but not necessarily that it is a wine of any great distinction (though it could be, sometimes).

Blanc de Blancs may describe any white wine made solely from white grapes, though usually the term is applied only to champagne. The phrase was first used in the Champagne region to distinguish wines made exclusively with the white Chardonnay grape from those produced from a combination of both black and white grapes (as most champagnes are). A true Blanc de Blancs will come from the Côte des Blancs, south of Epernay, and is often a light but particularly elegant and stylish wine.

Blending is the practice of 'marrying' or mixing wines of slightly different characteristics, ages or origins. Most (though not all) champagnes are blends; so is most port; so are virtually all sherries, even the finest. The practice — subject to extremely strict control under the Common Market wine laws, to prevent any abuses — is usually adopted for one of three main reasons:

1. As a means of producing a wine which will remain consistent in quality and style, year after year.
2. To create a wine which, in the aggregate, is better than any of the individual wines forming its ingredients.
3. At the bottom end of the scale, to help 'rescue' a very poor wine and turn it into one which is passable.

A really fine wine, like a château-bottled claret, is never a blend in this sense. On the other hand, it is only because of skilled blending that your favourite brand of sherry, however expensive or not, always has the same taste, bouquet, colour and style, whenever or wherever you buy it.

That applies equally to the big-selling ranges of low-priced branded table wines. Many of them were developed in accordance with market research: that is, leading wine firms conducted polls to establish what styles of wine most people preferred — e.g. sweet white with medium or light rather than heavy body, full rather than dry red — and then had blends made to meet those prevailing public tastes. So it is thanks to the practice of blending that you can rely on the absence of any unwanted change in the individual properties of each wine in such ranges.

Body is a term applied to a wine which feels 'heavy' on the tongue — a reflection of its alcohol content. A full body is an essential characteristic of a fine claret or Burgundy, and also of a great sweet white wine like Sauternes. For many other white wines, though, it's the last thing you'd want. The finesse and elegance of Moselles and champagnes, for example, would be spoilt by too much body.

Bouquet is the pleasing smell a wine gives off, a short interval after you open the bottle. It may remind you of fruit, herbs, flowers, or even just an echo of good rich earth brooding under the hot sun. In general, wines with the most pronounced bouquets are: those made in difficult soil, where the vines' tough fight for survival tends to bring out their best qualities; those with a high level of acidity; and, notably in northern vineyards, those produced from grapes which ripen slowly because they are not subject to excessively hot sunshine. By contrast, wines grown in easy conditions and hot temperatures have (though not always) much less distinctive bouquets. Professional wine buyers and other experts can often identify a wine, and even its age and class, just from sniffing its bouquet.

Bourgeois, in a wine context, is not at all the insult it has become when applied to humans. On the contrary, it could well be a high compliment. A 'bourgeois' claret, more often than not, is an excellent wine. In the Bordeaux region, the 'crus bourgeois' come next in line after the aristocratic 'classed growths' of the Médoc, Sauternes, St Emilion and Graves. So the term merely equates with

123

'middle class', in the old-fashioned sense, without derogatory overtones.

A good number of them, too, as frequently occurs in real life, have quite as much character and finesse as many of their social superiors (and even more, in some cases). Yet, generally, their prices are lower than the classed growth wines, particularly if you're prepared to buy them at an early stage and lay them down for three to four years. By the time they reach their peak, they will not only be wines of real distinction but will also have appreciated considerably in value.

Brut is the driest grade of all sparkling wines, notably champagne. In practice, a small, carefully-controlled amount of sweetening is added to almost all such wines. Even so, 'brut' on the label tells you that it's a lot drier than 'sec' (which means 'dry' but isn't particularly).

Cabinet is an anglicized version of Kabinett, a word originally used by German vineyard proprietors for wines they put aside for their own private use. Under the new German wine laws, it can be applied only to wines of the top grade and denotes a wine which is 'elegant, mature and of superior quality'. Not to be confused with Cabernet, which is one of the great grape varieties.

Character crops up in wine lists and auctioneers' patter as a descriptive term – e.g. 'a wine of undoubtful character' – which sometimes seems to come perilously close to the 'amused-at-its-presumption' nonsense that James Thurber poked fun at so effectively. To say that a wine has character, of course, is invariably taken to imply that it's a good one. But the point is that it does *not* always have to be rare or highly priced. You might well find wines of character at well below the £2 mark in your local supermarket.

For wine-tasting purposes, the phrase denotes much the

same — broadly speaking — as it does in human terms. If you describe someone as a 'character', you mean that he or she has unusually pronounced qualities of humour, good temper, straight thinking and talking, or whatever it may be . . . not necessarily eccentric or idiosyncratic, but undeniably distinctive. A wine of character may derive its distinguishing qualities from the particular grape varieties used in making it, from its specific geographical origin, or many other causes. From this it follows that the wine itself does not have to be a fine wine, or even specially outstanding, to deserve the compliment. What counts above all is that it should be 'interesting'.

Château-bottled — see Estate-bottled.

Corks have been used for centuries to stopper bottles. Although some inexpensive wines are now sealed with plastic 'corks' — and none the worse for it — a proper cork is essential for fine wines whose qualities will improve if they are left to age in bottle for some years. In fact, the quality of the cork and its actual length are often directly related to the anticipated lifespan of the wine it is to protect: for instance, you are likely to find the cork on a Beaujolais appreciably shorter than that on a great claret.

Cuvée (a blend) is derived from *cuve*, French for the tank or cask in which grapes are fermented during the wine-making process: the word is used to describe a specific batch or blend of grapes. The first pressing of grapes produces the finest wine; so when you see a wine described as *tête de cuvée*, you'll know that it's the best of its kind that the grower concerned is offering in any particular year.

Decanting may be required for venerable port or other fine old wines which throw a sediment in bottle. A crystal decanter always looks pretty on the dinner table but,

125

except for wines of this kind, the process isn't actually necessary for any others. Decanting needs great care if the sediment is not to be disturbed. The bottle should be opened gently and, with its mouth resting at a very slight angle in the mouth of the decanter, poured slowly until the first sign of sediment appears in the neck – easily seen if you put a lighted candle, or even a pocket torch, just behind the bottle. As an added precaution, you could also pass the wine through a fine strainer or a few layers of clean muslin. Incidentally, don't throw the sediment away. It may look unappetizing, but it is quite harmless and you can safely use it in cooking.

Demi-sec, literally translated, means 'half-dry'. But champagne or other sparkling wines described by the term will actually be pretty sweet. Another word denoting sweet, for such wines, is *doux*.

Denominazione di Origine Controllata (D.O.C. for short) is Italy's equivalent of Appellation Contrôlée and covers much the same kind of requirements – i.e. confirming that the wine was made within the district defined on the label, that it conforms to the characteristics and production techniques of the region, and so on. The very highest mark of status, for only a few of the finest Italian wines, will be D.O.C.G. (Denominazione di Origine Controllata e Garantita); but this is only 'in the pipeline' and has not yet been introduced at the time of writing.

Estate-bottled wines are made solely from a vineyard proprietor's own vines. By implication, bottling on the spot gives an assurance of quality and authenticity. It is standard procedure in Germany's best vineyards and in those of Bordeaux, where the term château-bottled is more often used. In Burgundy and the Côtes du Rhone, the equivalent wines are described as domaine-bottled.

Frizzante is an Italian wine term describing wines which, though not fully sparkling, have a slight natural tingle of 'prickle'. French wines of this sort are called *pétillant*; German and Austrian ones are termed *spritzig*.

Fruity, as a characteristic of wine, is not at all the same as 'grapey'. The former is nearly always a compliment; the latter is desirable only in a few specific cases. The majority of good young wines – notably those of Alsace, Beaujolais and most German white wines – remind you of fresh fruit in both their flavour and bouquet. It may be like plums, raspberries, even strawberries, but preferably it should not evoke the actual grapes – because wine with a pronounced flavour of the grapes from which it is made will usually lack subtlety and not be well balanced. Among exceptions, however, are the best wines made with Muscat grapes. These grapes almost invariably impart their special flavour to the aroma and taste, and the fact that they do so forms an integral part of such wines' particular charm.

Litre sizes of wine bottles are roughly equal to just over 1⅓ standard bottles. (At present, a standard bottle may vary from 70–75 centilitres, so an exact comparison is impossible but moves are afoot to fix it by law, eventually, at 75). As a further rule-of-thumb, the larger 1½-litre size is a fraction over two bottles and the 2-litre size is just under three standard bottles.

Manzanilla sherries come into the same category as Finos but can sometimes be even drier. They always have a slight salty tang.

Mousseux means 'foaming' and is the general French word for all sparkling wines, with one important exception, champagne. Though it certainly has plenty of foam, champagne is held to be in a class apart and is *never* described as a vin mousseux.

Nose is an alternative term used by wine tasters for a wine's bouquet or aroma. (Oddly enough, because they spend so much time sniffing the stuff, many professional tasters seem to develop pretty big noses themselves.)

Oloroso sherries, aromatic, full-bodied and darkest of the principal types already described earlier in the separate section on sherry, are also normally the basis of the so-called 'cream' or 'rich brown' sherries, blended in extra-sweet styles specifically for certain countries which happen to like them. They are often sold under appealing brand names. In Spanish, *oloroso* means scented or 'sweet-smelling' — and, quite apart from their taste, sherries of this type certainly are.

Pourriture noble is a French phrase meaning 'noble rot' and refers to a mould — formal name, *Botrytis cinerea* — which forms on the skins of ripening grapes in various wine districts, especially those producing the great white wines of Sauternes and the Rhine Valley. The mould is 'noble' because it is responsible for the supremely high quality of the wines concerned. Its spores suck water from the juice until the grapes become shrivelled and brown; in consequence, the almost glycerine-like juice retains a bigger proportion of sugar to water than is usual. So the beneficent parasite, without leaving any mouldy taste of its own in the white wine it affects, can take the credit for their extra sweetness and luscious flavour.

QbA and QmP are the initials habitually used for the top two of the three classifications into which all German wines are divided (and which must always be shown clearly on the bottle labels). The full list, as laid down by Germany's wine laws, is:

1. Deutscher Tafelwein — table wine of good quality.
2. QbA — Qualitatswein bestimmter Anbaugebiete —

denoting quality wines from specified districts, made from defined grape varieties and subject to close official control during production.

3. QmP — Qualitatswein mit Pradikat, the best grade. Much like France's Appellation Contrôlée, the 'Pradikat' certifies officially that (as with QbA) the wines concerned come from strictly defined districts, are made only from specified types of grapes, and are subject to inspection and approval by government experts before they can be sold.

Both QbA and QmP wines are also given a code number to identify them, printed on each label; but only the QmP group is entitled to display the additional indications of specially high quality used by German wine growers, such as *spätlese* and *auslese* (wines made from late-picked grapes and appreciably sweeter and more elegant than the standard types).

Quinta (pronounced 'keenta') is a Portuguese word for a vineyard estate and is most often seen on the labels of port bottles, since it tends to be used like a brand name. In a wine sense, it's roughly equivalent to the words château, or domaine, in France. And, like them, it carries its own implication that wines allowed to bear its name are of high quality.

Racking is the process whereby young wine is drawn off carefully from one vat to another, after fermentation, to separate it from its lees and sediment, which are left at the bottom of the first cask. Although this entails a loss of 2—3 % of the wine's volume, it is the only way to ensure that the fermented wine becomes bright and unclouded. All well-made wines, therefore, will be racked at least twice — and some as many as four times — before they are bottled.

Rounded wines are just what you would expect from the word: well-balanced, complete and without any obvious faults. The wine in question needn't necessarily be a particularly great or expensive one — but you could never apply the adjective to a poor one.

Sommelier — a posh word for a wine waiter. In fact, though, the Guild of Sommeliers does a jolly good job in arranging lectures, wine visits and tastings for its members, to help ensure that they really do know their stuff.

Spätlese means 'late harvest' and describes high-quality German wines made from grapes picked some time after those harvested for the normal vintage. Being more fully ripened, the grapes produce fuller-bodied and sweeter wines than the standard wines from the same vineyard. Even richer are *Auslese* wines, for which the bunches of late-picked grapes are specially selected, all imperfect grapes being removed before the pressing. Rarest and most expensive of all are *Beerenauslese* and *Trockenbeerenauslese* wines. The former are made from individually chosen grapes affected by the beneficient 'noble rot' fungus (see *Pourriture noble*, above), the latter from selected grapes left on the vines until the 'noble rot' has shrivelled them up almost like raisins.

Spumante is an Italian word which means sparkling or foaming and, when applied to wines, describes those which have a full-blooded sparkle (as opposed to the mild tingle of *frizzante* wines). Italy's best-known sparkling wines — for example, Asti Spumante — come from the prolific wine-growing region near Turin, in the north-west. The finest are made by the 'champagne method'. Most spumante wines have low alcoholic strength and tend to be on the sweet side.

Tannin is the secret behind the practice of some home-made wine enthusiasts who, when fermenting their fruit-based concoctions, add in a couple of dollops of cold tea. The point is that tannin, as found in tea, is an important factor of most real wines, particularly reds like claret. I should stress that my use of the word 'real' is not intended to be pejorative. Although personally I'm interested solely in the genuine article there are estimated to be around 1,000,000 amateur wine and beer makers in Britain alone – and I've tasted some home brews that were undoubtedly both interesting and pleasant. My only reservation is that such wines should always be appraised to their own right and on their own terms, without silly attempts to equate them directly with Burgundy, Bordeaux or whatever.

While wines with a high proportion of tannin have a mouth-puckering astringency, the important role played by the substance is that it helps to keep them in good condition, thus contributing to their longevity. The organic compounds which make up tannin are found in oak-bark and in the wood, stems and roots of numerous plants. In wine, it comes mainly from the pips, stalks and skins of the grapes; a certain amount is picked up from the wood, too, when wines are matured in new oak casks.

The more tannin a top quality young wine contains, the longer it will take to reach its peak – and the longer it will live. Fortunately, though, the taste of tannin becomes much less pronounced with age, because it forms part of the sediment thrown by fine red wines as they mature. That's why older clarets, especially, are less astringent than young ones.

V.D.Q.S. stands for Vins Délimités de Qualité Supérieure and, like Appellation Contrôlée, is an officially-backed guarantee that the wines concerned come from a specific area, are made only with the approved grape varieties, and meet the regulations regarding maximum yield per acre, traditional local production methods, and so on. Although V.D.Q.S. is regarded as just below A.C. in status, it is still a difficult distinction to obtain and the wines are anything but second-rate. Indeed, before qualifying for the classification, they have to be tasted and approved by a committee of impartial experts.

Wine Routes. When motoring on the Continent, look out for signs to the *Route du Vin* (in France) or *Weinstrasse* (in Germany). Both phrases mean 'wine route' and driving along these back roads — always in superb countryside — is the best possible way to get to know the picturesque wine-growing villages of the districts concerned. Probably the most renowned French wine route is in Alsace, meandering through a string of beautiful medieval townships, nearly all of which have special cellars where you can taste their local wines.

VINTAGES — WHAT AND WHY?

There is a widely-held misconception that vintage wines are, almost automatically, exceptionally good ones. In fact, *every* year is a 'vintage' year. The word simply denotes the annual grape harvest and the particular wine made from it.

Small wonder, then that one of the puzzles confronting the newcomer to wine-drinking is the distinction between vintage and non-vintage wines . . . why some are classed as vintage and other are not. The immediate answer is that a bottle of vintage wine has a label showing the year of its birth. So, by implication, the label is usually a mark of higher quality. It denotes a wine made in one year, whereas non-vintage bottles don't display any particular date (and, in fact, usually contain blends of wine from several different years).

But there's more to it than that. To find out how much more, I asked experts at some of the top British wine houses for their own explanations.

Expert No. 1 began by quoting the great connoisseur

André Simon, whose definition of the chief difference between the two was that dated (vintage) wines show greater promise of improving with age and should be kept for later consumption, whereas undated (non-vintage) wines are ready for immediate consumption and may, but need not, be kept.

Another expert pointed out: 'The majority of wine that is sold is at the *ordinaire* level. Huge gallonages are produced and marketed cheaply, with never a hint of a vintage on the label. Many of these wines are very good, of their type, and certainly they offer the newcomer an excellent introduction to wine-drinking.

'Compared with the best vintage wines, however, it's

'He can not only tell you the vintage but who trod the grapes.'

rather like the distinction between, say, mass-produced clothes and a hand-made suit. The former obviously have to meet acceptable and often quite high standards if they're to find ready buyers; but the latter costs more and, like all products which require individual attention, is not available in big quantities and takes longer to bring to perfection. So it follows that it is only with the more expensive wines that one identifies their village of origin or the label, or even the property or the grower. And at this level of quality, one adds the date of birth to the pedigree.'

The number of people who buy fine vintage wines is only a tiny percentage of the total wine-drinking public. 'But there must always be such *vin de garde* – wines for the keeping – because ultimately the newcomer to wine-drinking will acquire a more discerning palate and will want to try better things,' said my first expert.

'Most of us, when going by train, have to travel second-class. Most of us would like to travel first-class – and surely this is what a vintage wine is all about?

'There will never be a shortage of people wanting to travel first-class, even if fares go sky-high. Prices of the latest Premier Cru clarets, for instance, are now rarely below about £12 a bottle, and often very much more – yet there are still people who will buy such wines at such prices.'

Fortunately, there are still plenty of fine wines at rather more accessible levels. Otherwise, it would be difficult indeed for the average wine-drinker to graduate to what eventually becomes one of the most fascinating aspects of vintage wines – detecting the slight variations shown by a particular wine in separate years.

One British expert described it as 'distinguishing between different individuals of the same family'. Citing a famous claret very popular with informed wine-drinkers, he said: 'As an example, you will find that, although they have many characteristics in common, Calon Segur 1973 is a different individual from Calon Segur 1972. This adds

134

to the interest of drinking, because one is then led to a much finer involvement in the subtleties of taste.'

'A further advantage of recording a wine's date of birth,' he said, 'is that it helps greatly in watching the maturation of an individual wine over the years.'

This careful differentiation of vintage wines, and the watch on their respective progress as they gradually improve towards their peak, is not simply a 'mystique' of the trade. Eventually, it is of direct benefit to the consumer as well. Because of it, you can be sure that vintage bottles will be sold to you only when they are ready for drinking. That may be a question of minimum standards, for many of such wines might well become even better if kept for a few more years. After all, a really great claret can live for a century or more. But at least you have the assurance, when a vintage wine comes on to the market, that it will never be *below* a recognized standard.

Longevity is also a feature of great vintage port. One of the experts I consulted told me that he had recently been privileged to sample an 1848 port which he said was still 'fighting fit'.

Vintage port and champagne, however, have one salient difference from other fine wines. Both are usually formed of blends, whereby the makers seek to maintain — every year — the same qualities for which their product won renown originally. With port, in particular, you will rarely be able to buy bottles containing wine from one year alone. What happens, therefore, is that each house declares a vintage in any given year only when it considers that its product is exceptionally good that year. It is an individual matter; even with neighbouring vineyards, growers will not always produce a vintage port at the same time. On average, the best port houses declare a vintage about three times in each decade.

As my final expert put it: 'Since the vagaries of climate represent the principal variable influencing the devel-opment of the grape harvest, a vintage wine can be of exceptional quality if that year's weather conditions have been favourable. In another year, the wines may have to be produced under conditions which are far from ideal. So the declaration of a port or champagne vintage does denote a wine of quality, because it is made only from those wines produced under favourable conditions.'

That, in fact, could be regarded as the key to all vintage wines. But with one cautionary rider. . . . Those tables showing Good, Average or Below-average vintage assessments for various types of wine may be handy as a general guide. They should never be regarded as gospel, though, for *all* the wines from a given region in any one year. Since dramatic changes of climate occur within even quite small areas, a few vineyards may well have produced good wines in an otherwise poor year – and naturally the opposite may also apply sometimes.

WHAT TO LOOK FOR ON A WINE LABEL

Since September 1977, new Common Market wine laws have been in force, designed to protect the consumer by laying down the way — within the E.E.C. area, anyway — that table wines and other still light wines should be described and presented on the bottle labels (and also in price lists, advertising and so on).

At first sight, a few of the provisions look horrifically bureaucratic and complex, and I have to admit that one or two of them struck me as unduly pernickety: for instance, the fact that (broadly speaking) only the ordinary, still, light wines from E.E.C. countries may be described as 'table wine', whereas most of those from other areas (with some quality or geographical exceptions) must simply be called 'wine'.

However, as so often happens, the changes are a good deal less complicated in practice than they seem on paper. And for you and me, when buying wine, their effect is entirely beneficial. For the basic object of the whole exercise is to help ensure that we get the exact wine we pay for, and to provide all the information we will find useful when deciding which to buy.

The new regulations, therefore, specify certain details which *must* be included in the information given on the label (or wine list), as well as various other details which are permitted optionally. The former include the country of origin, the name and address of the bottler, the nominal volume of the wine, and measures designed to avoid confusion between quality and lesser wines; the latter cover such points as colour or type, alcoholic strength, and brand names (again provided these don't cause confusion or convey a false impression).

Many of the requirements merely echo what was already prevailing practice among most wine producers and merchants. However, one minor example of the kind of changes entailed is provided by one of the world's biggest selling light, dry white wines, which was formerly known as Yugoslav Riesling, but now has to be described as Yugloslav Laski Riesling. This may seem an unnecessarily fussy point of detail, but its purpose is to make clear that the Riesling grape variety used for the Yugoslav wine is not the same as the famed Rhine Riesling grape from which Germany's hocks and Moselles are grown.

Most people buying a bottle of plonk for the weekend couldn't care less about such differentiations, I imagine. But it's a case of 'them as can read, let 'em read'. For, as newcomers to wine begin to learn more about the subject, they look increasingly to the information on the labels — small print included — to tell them precisely what to expect from the bottle's contents. And that, of course, is what the new labelling regulations are all about.

In future, the permitted and mandatory descriptions of a wine will offer us extra safeguards. Not just against fraud (because, despite occasional alarmist stories, it really is very rare in the wine trade as a whole), but above all against terms and expressions which could — however unintentionally — mislead the casual buyer or confuse him into thinking that a table wine is in fact a quality wine. When the details given are properly interpreted, in short, the distinction between various categories of wine should now be clear-cut and unambiguous.

As an example of the four kinds of detail which are now mandatory, the label might say that it's a table wine from France bottled by Messrs. X and that the bottle was filled with 72 cl of wine. In addition, among the wide range of optional information allowed, the label might also specify that it's a red wine, medium-dry, goes well with certain meats, and how strong it is.

Put those two sets of information together and the facts at your disposal are that the bottle contains a red table wine from France, bottled by Messrs. X, medium-dry and excellent with roast meat or game, 72 cl in nominal volume and with an alcoholic strength of 12°. In short, the overall effect is nothing like as complicated as one might fear, its upshot simply being to provide more than adequate information to help you choose which wine you want, and with the added comfort that the new regulations ensure the details stated are completely reliable.

The various markings and other aspects of the regulations offer the consumer a further hidden guarantee. If there is any complaint about a bottle of wine or its contents, it is now possible to trace the wine right back to its origins, to see what has happened to it at each different stage in its career, and thereby to establish whether it is genuinely what the label states it to be.

We can now be as certain as it is reasonably possible to be that the table wine we think we have bought is the one we are actually getting. Clearly, this reassurance ought to apply equally to other types of wine. Similar regulations, therefore, are in the pipeline for both fortified and sparkling wines.

Also envisaged, long term, is the standardization of ordinary bottle sizes, which at present vary from about 70 cl to 75 cl in content. These discrepancies are an undoubted cause for complaint against the trade and their eradication must surely be to everyone's advantage. The sooner the better, I reckon.

Here is a broad guide to how some of the new wine labels should now look. The examples on the left, in each pair, show the facts which *must* be given; those on the right illustrate both the obligatory information and a selection from the wide range of additional details also permitted.

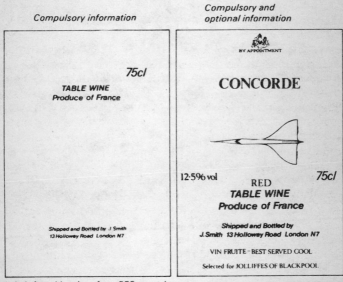

Labels for table wines from EEC countries.

Further details may also be given, optionally, for wines described by reference to their geographical area of production.

APPELLATION CHABLIS CONTROLEE

Bottled by
FELIX K. WITGENSTEIN AND CO. LTD.
BOW VAULTS LONDON EC3

PRODUCE OF FRANCE   75cl

1976
CARLTON CLUB
FOURCHAUME

premier cru

Grand Vin Blanc

produced from the pinot chardonnay grape.

APPELLATION CHABLIS CONTROLEE

12% vol   **PRODUCE OF FRANCE**   75cl

Bottled by
FELIX K. WITGENSTEIN AND CO. LTD.
BOW VAULTS LONDON EC3

Boullez et Cie
Negociant à Dijon

EEC quality wine psr

Specimen label for EEC quality wines.

75cl

SPANISH WINE

Bottled by J Smith 123 Holloway Road London N7

by appointment

VILLA ROSA
RED

SPANISH WINE

11% vol   75cl

Bottled by J Smith 123 Holloway Road London N7

Selected for Jolliffes of Blackpool

Shippers Don Quixote
Avenida Madona 2133 Bilbao

Specimen label for 'third country' wines.

For 'third country' wines, originating from countries outside the E.E.C., the compulsory information is similar — except that ordinary wines must not be described as 'table wines' but simply as 'wine'; and if they are not bottled in a Common Market country, the name and address of the importer has to be shown.

142

Wine
Cups and Mulls

Depending on the season, wine can be served in two special ways which are invariably a big hit when you're entertaining. In summer, no drink is more refreshing for your guests than one of the delicious wine coolers, made principally with light wines and mixtures of fruit. In the cold winter months, none is more welcome than one of the warming, spicy mulled wines, which immediately evoke thoughts of Dickens and the best traditions of Old England.

Whether cup or mull, neither is difficult to make. And both have the advantage that, depending on which recipes you choose, you can use quite inexpensive wines for them.

Here are the Nimmo family favourites:

CUPS

Claret cup — for 10 glasses
2 bottles claret, 85g (3 oz) sugar, 1.4 dl (¼ pt) water, 2 oranges, 2 lemons, soda water, ice, cucumber slices, sprigs of mint, sliced apple or orange.

Method: Boil the sugar and water with the rinds of the oranges and lemons. Squeeze the juice of the fruit and pour in the claret. Put the ice in a bowl and pour the wine mixture over it. Add the soda water just before serving and float slices of cucumber, apple, orange and sprigs of mint on the surface.

White wine cup — for 20 glasses
2 bottles dry or medium-dry white wine, 1 miniature bottle Maraschino or Cointreau, 1 large bottle tonic water, 1 small bottle lemonade, 1 orange (sliced), 1 lemon (sliced), slices of cucumber.

Method: Put all the ingredients into a large bowl and place it in the fridge for one hour before it is required. Serve with ice cubes.

Fiesta punch — for 22 glasses
2 bottles sweet white wine, 1 large bottle soda water, ¾ cup sugar, sliced fruit (oranges, maraschino cherries etc.) 1 large tin unsweetened pineapple juice, lemon juice, ice.

Method: In a punch bowl, dissolve the sugar in half a cup of lemon juice and pineapple juice, well chilled. Add two bottles of chilled wine and ice cubes. Before serving, pour in the soda water and garnish with the fruit.

Sangria — for 24 glasses
2 bottles red wine, sliced apples, oranges, lemons and peaches, 2 large bottles soda water, ice.

Method: Add the wine to the fruit and put the mixture into the fridge for at least an hour. Add the soda water and ice immediately before serving.

Riesling Cup — for 30 glasses
3 bottles Yugoslav Riesling, 1 bottle dry cider, 1 large bottle lemonade, slices of orange, lemon and a sprig of mint.

Method: Chill the liquid ingredients in the fridge, stir them together and add the fruit and mint.

Dry white wine cup — for 32 glasses
3 bottles cheap dry white wine, 1 bottle bianco vermouth, 1 large bottle lemonade. Slices of lemon, orange and a sprig of mint.

Method: Chill the liquid ingredients in the fridge, mix them together, and add the fruit and mint.

Rhine wine cup — for 65—70 glasses
6 bottles Rhine wine, 1 bottle dry vermouth, 1 bottle dry cider, 2 large bottles of lemonade, ½ bottle orange curaçao, slices of orange and lemon, and a sprig of mint.

Method: Chill the liquid ingredients in the fridge, mix them together and add the fruit and mint.

See that the wines are well chilled before being mixed, but don't freeze them or the cup will lose any taste except one of coldness. A large block of ice will dissolve much more slowly than small pieces and there will therefore be less dilution of the wine if a big chunk is used in the wine cup. When making ice yourself, take out the separator in the freezing tray to give you a large block.

The appearance of the cup is very important, and herbs add much as finishing touches. Borage, mint, balm, sweet-scented verbena and lemon mint are often used.

If soda water is added to the wine cup, it should be at the last minute. If the wine mixture is not sweet enough, you can add sugar, but a little liqueur is better still. If it's too sweet, a glass of dry sherry will sharpen it. From time to time stir the cup well from the bottom to make sure that it is evenly flavoured.

If the wine cup runs low, it can always be topped up with lemonade or soda water. When using lemon, peel the rind thinly and don't use the pith, besides being bitter, it will dissolve and cloud the drink.

MULLS

Port and lemon mull — for 12 glasses
1 bottle port, 2 lemons, cloves, ½ litre (1 pint) boiling water, 56g (2 oz) lump sugar, mixed spices.

Method: Stick the cloves into a lemon and warm it in the oven at 176° C (350° F) for 15 minutes. Pour the bottle of port into a saucepan and bring it nearly to the boil. Boil the water, adding a good pinch of spices, then add the boiled water with the spices and the baked lemon to the wine. Rub lumps of sugar on to the rind of the other lemon, then put the sugar into a bowl, adding half the juice of the lemon, and pour this into the hot wine mixture. Serve really hot.

Negus — for 18 glasses
1 bottle Cyprus sherry, 1 litre (2 pints) boiling water, 1 lemon, 1 miniature bottle brandy, nutmeg, sugar.

Method: Warm the Cyprus sherry in a saucepan very slowly, slice and add the lemon, then pour in the boiling water. Add a little grated nutmeg, sugar to taste, and lastly the brandy.

Christmas cheer — for 30 glasses
4 bottles red wine, ½ litre (1 pint) water, ¼ bottle dark rum, 1 lemon, 12 cloves, ½ teaspoon ground cinnamon, nutmeg.

Method: Heat the wine, water and run together, stick the lemon with cloves and bake in the oven for 15 minutes at 176° C (350° F). Add the cinnamon and a little grated nutmeg to the wine mixture, then float the hot cloved lemon in it.

Firecracker — for 8 glasses
1 bottle full red wine, 2 cups water, 1 cup granulated sugar, 2 lemons, 4 small sticks cinnamon, 4 cloves.

Method: Boil the water with the sugar, lemon juice, cinnamon and cloves for five minutes. Add the wine and heat slowly to boiling point, but do not actually boil.

Dr Johnson's Choice — for 25 glasses
A very old and popular mull of the eighteenth century. 1 litre bottle claret, 1 sliced orange, 12 lumps sugar, 6 cloves, ½ litre (1 pint) water, nutmeg, 1 wine glass brandy.

Method: Pour the claret into a saucepan and add the orange slices, sugar and cloves. Bring almost to the boil. Boil the water and pour it into the mixture. Add the brandy, then pour the mull into warmed glasses and grate nutmeg on top of each.

Spanish bollan — for 12 glasses
1 litre Spanish red wine, 1 cup sugar, grated nutmeg, lemon slices.

Method: Heat the wine, sugar and nutmeg to almost boiling point, then pour it into glasses with a slice of lemon in each.

Guy Fawkes — for 12 glasses
1 bottle red wine, 1 miniature bottle brandy, ½ litre (1 pint) hot water, 12 lumps sugar, cloves, nutmeg, 1 orange, sliced.

Method: Pour the wine into the saucepan and add to it the orange, sugar and cloves. Bring the contents of the pan nearly to the boil. Boil the water and add it to the other ingredients. Add the brandy, then pour the mixture into glasses and add a little grated nutmeg to the top of each.

It is important that a mull is served really hot, but never boiled, otherwise the alcohol will evaporate. To make your mull, you need (apart from the ingredients) one 3–4.5-litre (6-8-pint) saucepan or a preserving pan. Or even better, have two large pans so that one is always on the brew. You also need a plastic funnel and ordinary wine glasses. If you do not have enough glasses for your party, you can often hire them from wine merchants, who will sometimes even lend them to you for free if your wine order is large enough. To prevent glasses from cracking when pouring a hot mull into them, either warm them first, or place a spoon in each while pouring in the hot wine. At an informal party, the mull can be served with a ladle straight from the saucepan. Or the wine can be ladled from a warmed punch bowl or tureen.

Use inexpensive wines to make the cup. Where claret or Burgundy are mentioned in traditional recipes a similar style of red wine is equally suitable.

Ale and Hearty

I cannot say that I am any kind of beer expert. I have a friend who will literally travel miles on a pilgrimage to drink a particular beer, but I can't pretend that I am ever tempted to join him. I cannot identify beers one from another but I don't drink beer a great deal. I have to confess that I only really drink beer when I'm frantically thirsty. For example, when I was crossing the Flinders Range in Australia recently, I hadn't had a glass of beer for almost twelve months, but having tramped across this very hot, arid, extraordinary volcanic basin, I knew there was only one drink in the world that would be suitable for that particular moment: a glass of refrigerated Australian beer!

Having confessed that I don't drink beer that often, you won't be surprised when I tell you that it has never crossed my mind to actually make it myself. As far as I am concerned, home-brewing is a hobby fraught with dangers. But my having admitted that I'm no authority on beer doesn't mean that you should skip this chapter. Far from it. Fortunately for me (and for you) I have a friend called Arthur Binsted who knows all there is to know about beer and he has done his very best to educate me. Arthur is a former Chairman of the British Bottlers' Institute and holds Fellowship Diplomas covering beer and cidar as well as all sorts of other interesting drinks, and what he doesn't know about ale isn't worth knowing.

THE BIRTH OF BEER

Imagine the scene. It is Babylonia and the date is 6000 B.C. Agriculture is settled in these parts and new-fangled

'He's lived in this village for forty years but never really belonged.'

barley is a novel food crop. No one knows about beer because it hasn't yet been invented. In fact, it is on this very day that the liquid miracle will take place. The head of a Babylonian household is looking into one of his Ali Baba-like jars of barley. Let us peer into the jar with him. Oh dear! It seems to have got some water in it. And it's warm. The man is about to yell at his wives but he tastes the tepid bubbling liquid first. He has to admit it's rather good. What has happened?

With hindsight, it is easy enough to tell. Down there in Babylonia, where they used to be in the hanging-garden business, some barley was moistened in its jar and the sun got at it and warmed it. The barleycorns thought spring had come, so they set about building up their enzymes with which to break down the rock-hard stock of starch in the husk. For if the embryo was to be fed it could not just be left to try to ingest the starch; the molecular structure is too great for a barley embryo's digestion. So a scattering of enzymes, like salt on Sunday lunch, made it all digestible — in this case by converting the starch to easily assimilable sugars.

Fortunately for all of us, on this particular occasion, this did not happen to barleycorns in the ground in springtime but to those in a pot in hot weather. The sun continued to warm the pot until the conversion process stopped, leaving all the goodness still in the solution. Today this is done scientifically and is closely controlled so that dry malted barleycorns can be offered. We call it malting.

Malting

Malting prepares the grain for the brewer to mix it with hot liquor (brewers always call water liquor; no reason for it — they just always have), so that the goodness in the grain is soaked out, rather like making an outsize pot of tea. The resulting liquid is called wort. Which, for some inscrutable reason is pronounced wert — but, again, it always has been, so who are we to interfere?

Having extracted the goodness from the grain, the wort is sent to the copper where it is boiled and hops are added.

Hops

There are something like 1500 different brands of beer in the United Kingdom, Australasia and North America. They range from darkest stout to palest lager or light ale. The variations are all on a single theme: the basic brewing process which is the same for all of them. The variety begins with the choice of barley malt. Barley, grown in fields and subjected to the weather, can vary almost infinitely in its properties, its flavour and character. In malting, it can be encouraged to subtlety or to a healthily rounded flavour, and it can be varied in colour during the heating which is the final stage of the malting process.

The brewer has a wide selection of malts with which to achieve the character he wants in his beer. He often completes the variety by adding small quantities of other grain, giving what is known as a mixed grist for the mashing stage. In Britain, the brewers have for centuries practised the art of the mixed grist, led by the Saxon monks who contributed greatly to our knowledge of brewing in the Middle Ages. The earliest known written recipe, providing for the use of a mixed grist of barley malt, oats and so on, is dated around 1240 and comes from the Priory of Worcester.

The brewer's job begins with the selection of malts — he probably blends them to achieve the desired result — and the choice of the many varieties of hops. The hops are added to beer only to flavour it and are nothing to do with the quality or the body of the beer. They can impart a wonderfully wide variety of flavours and aromas: hop oils have something like 2000 aromatic substances in them. A gas chromatograph would probably provide the wallpaper for an average-size suburban villa — if one wanted that kind of wallpaper.

Hops came late into British brewing. They were unknown in Britain until 1400 and were not widely adopted for another hundred years or so. Until the sixteenth century, if English ale was flavoured at all it was with domestic herbs. Around that time, the unhopped beverage was known as ale while the hopped variety was called beer, from *bière*, because hops were imported from Flanders. In fact, the Romans used to chew hops in about the first century A.D. but this was to give them an appetite. Nowadays, all ales and beers are hopped, so that the distinction has disappeared.

From the gent in Babylonia who got his barley wet and found he had produced malt and ale by accident, the knowledge of barley and of brewing moved steadily westward. There is excellent pictorial evidence of chaps in ancient Egypt, about 2000 years further on, brewing. We know they were ancient Egyptians because they had bird-like eyes in the sides of their heads and we know they were brewing because they were doing it as we do it today — save that in those days, if they wanted any heavy work done, they raided surrounding tribes and brought in some slaves to do it for them. The paintings and drawings show that the Egyptians of those days not only drank ale but they revered it, using it in worship and medicine.

The liquor

The type of water used for brewing also affects the flavour and character of the end-product. In Britain we are singularly fortunate because those same Saxon monks in the Middle Ages discovered a great many of the sources of liquor which are still in use today. Burton-on-Trent, with its water simply bursting at the seams with the kind of salts wanted for the ales that come from those parts, is a classic example.

153

So important is the character of Burton water that for Burton-type ales some brewers use the well-recognized 'burtonizing' salts in their brewing water, and these salts are used by some brewers in other countries.

Fermentation

Having established that the barley malt, the other grains, the flavouring hops and the brewing liquor itself all combine to give the final character to the beer, it is time to look at the wort boiling in the copper where we left it. Having boiled it briskly for about a couple of hours — brewers are pernickety about the length of boiling time and each has his own ideas — the brewer next puts the wort through a cooler to bring it down to around room temperature.

Now comes the tricky bit: adding a pure yeast culture so that the fermentation can start. This yeast culture is guarded with the greatest care, being kept in aseptic conditions so that no wild yeast or other intruder can gain access to it. It is of great importance that the yeast culture be pure to ensure that the character of the beer is consistent. Similarly, for the fermentation pattern to run true, the temperature of the fermenting wort also needs control, which is why there are coils in the fermenting vessels.

In days gone by, fermentation was carried out in open vessels and the air in the room was kept as pure as possible. In recent years a great many brewers have gone over to closed fermenting vessels, so that there can be close control of purity, of temperature and all the other necessary factors.

Once the primary fermentation is over, it is time to decide the form of packaging into which the finished beer is to go. Supposing we are going to sell some of it as cask-conditioned beer, we rack it into the casks (how 'to rack' came to mean 'to fill' no one knows, but it does), add a jug of priming solution (priming sugar and water) and some isinglass finings, keep it in the brewery for a day or so and send it to the pubs. Here it is stillaged, a tap goes into the head of the cask (the end towards the cellarman) and a spile goes into the bung on top. This beer now goes through its secondary fermentation, using as food for the yeast the priming sugar added at the brewery. The spile (first hard then soft), controls the emission of carbon dioxide and when the fermentation has finished the isinglass finings slowly descend through the beer, carrying down the yeast cells, bits of hops and other debris, leaving a clear beer.

While this has been going on, the rest of that batch has been undergoing its secondary fermentation at the brewery; clarified by fining or filtration or both, and the beer can be packaged. Most of this brewery-conditioned beer is sold from kegs or in bottles or cans. The filling of all these containers is done basically in the same way. First, the container is filled with carbon dioxide, a gas which is the by-product of fermentation. This drives out the air. Next, the beer is flowed into the container, displacing the carbon dioxide, so that the beer is up to the required level and the headspace of the vessel is filled with the carbon dioxide. This means there is no air in the package. The absence of air means that the beer will not oxidize because there is no oxygen present, and other impurities which can be introduced by air will also be kept out of the container. So the shelf-life of this kind of beer is probably several months, as distinct from days with a cask which serves beer by air displacement. Neither type of beer is inferior to the other but the cask beer has a much shorter shelf-life and tends to lose its natural carbonation.

On the other hand, some keg beers — because they retain their carbonation — are thought by a few people to be 'fizzy'. Nonetheless, these beers are still excellent products and were responsible for rescuing the beer industry in the United Kingdom from the doldrums of the late 1950s. At that time, production had fallen below 24 million barrels a year and the selection of beers available in pubs was far less than it is today. People — many of them — wanted brighter, more cheerful beers to go with their post-war mood. By introducing keg beers (first perfected in the 1930s) alongside cask beers, brewers succeeded in pleasing their customers to the extent that sales of bottled beer fell away from about 40 % of the market in the late 1950s to today's 20 % or so. During that time the total brew has gone up to over 40 million barrels.

Without question, the great phenomenon in the beer industry in recent years has been the growth of lager, from 9.9 % of the market in 1971 to 14.9 % in 1973 and 24.7 % in 1977. It brought with it a mammoth problem for brewers to solve. This arose out of the fact that ale can be produced in a lager brewery but, except at extra cost and trouble, lager cannot normally be produced in an ale brewery. So brewers had to decide whether to let this demand for lager be met from Continental sources, or to go into lager production for themselves on a far larger scale than before — and at today's engineering prices for equipment and buildings. Fortunately, British brewers decided to produce their own lagers and it is estimated that the U.K. production of lager has for some years been saving Britain about £300 millions each year in terms of balance of payments.

THE BIRTH OF THE BREWERIES

Until about 300 years ago each inn or pub brewed its own beer, but gradually the innkeepers realized that some of their number were significantly better at the brewing job than others. There being comparatively little hampering legislation to stop them, the more proficient ones began to sell beer in casks to the less able and this was, in many cases, the origin of breweries as we know them today.

156

In 1640 or 1642 — there seems to be some doubt about the exact date since both of these years are mentioned in the literature — Oliver Cromwell, self-styled Lord-Protector of England, set about raising money to pay for the Civil War he was waging against Charles I by levying a tax of one shilling and threepence on each barrel of beer brewed. By the end of the Protectorate the beer tax had already been doubled.

After the restoration of the monarchy under Charles II the tax gatherers soon appreciated that it was easier to collect larger sums of what was now called the beer duty from fewer places than it had been to get it from every inn and alehouse, so they strongly encouraged the growth of breweries. After all, in those days the best way to collect money was to send a file of soldiers, fully armed and escorting a treasure chest, to each point of collection. It was a slow and cumbrous process but at least most of the money reached the national coffers safely.

Another reason for the establishment of breweries was the fact that brewing was and is an expensive production process which meant it was far cheaper to brew centrally and create an efficient distribution system. In the natural course of events, this soon extended to serving countries overseas. There was the expanding British Empire with thousands of men and women serving abroad. And to serve this Empire (and to bring home some of the fruits of the expatriates' efforts!) a large mercantile fleet had come into being, ranging from the tea-clippers under sail to steamers and later even the oil-fired ships. Since these ships were calling on British people in various countries, it was logical to take British ale and beer to them. Two problems arose — and one solved the other. Beer could not possibly survive the heat of the tropics in the normal course of shipping. On the other hand, British beer had long been among the cheapest in the world, so to keep it that way it could not be burdened with a high shipping tariff. For many years the answer was found in shipping casks of ale right down in the bilges, where it travelled as paying ballast, at a very low cost to the shipper. Being so low down – often far below the water line – the beer travelled through the tropical areas, such as the Suez Canal and the Red Sea, or down the west coast of Africa, at a practically equable temperature all the way.

A curious fact arose out of this. India was for a long time one of the best customers for the brewers, because of the size of the British military and civil contingents, and the particular kind of beer shipped to them soon became known as India Pale Ale, today known by its initials I.P.A. There are written accounts of some brewers finding that this kind of beer matured so well in the holds of Indiamen that they sent some of it on the round trip to Bombay and back, then selling it at home as India Pale Ale. It built a fine reputation for itself. It seems likely that the steady temperature and the long, slow rocking movement of the casks in the holds kept the yeast remaining in the casks well mixed with all the beer, achieving a slow and even secondary fermentation throughout the whole voyage. Today, the several brewery companies which produce I.P.A. find a ready sale for it both on draught and in bottle.

One of the great countries to emerge from the old Empire was, of course, Australia, and in the early days of the then Colony, the people relied in great measure for necessities as well as luxuries upon the ships that came out from home. After the seeds and the spuds and the stud animals and all the rest – including those rabbits! – there was always the great moment when hogsheads of British ale were hauled on to the deck and lowered into the boats for the short trip ashore. Once on the beach, a ship's officer held an auction for the sale of each hogshead. The ale had been bought by the captains or by the ships' owners and this beach auction recompensed them for the expenditure of their 'risk capital'. Not a very great risk when one thinks about it. Soon, brewery companies grew in Australia and showed themselves well able to cater for

158

the needs of their population. The close link with Britain was undoubtedly the major factor in making Australia an ale-drinking country, but while in Britain around a quarter of the market today is in lager, Australia has now changed over virtually completely to this type of beer.

BEER BY-PRODUCTS

By-products from breweries are full of good things. In addition to the spent grain used for cattle feed, many brewers find a ready market for spent hops among

'Wonderful news, Sarah, the doctor's put me back on Guinness!'

horticulturists, who use it as mulch. Normally, it is purchased by processors who first chop it into a form more readily usable by the growers; many gardeners believe hop mulch is the finest thing for their roses and many have first-class roses to prove it.

Even more interesting is the production of yeast. At the end of each brew, there is about four to five times as much yeast as the quantity originally 'pitched' into the brew. Brewing yeast is a most carefully controlled and pure culture. It is first pressed at the brewery to dry it and is then sold to manufacturers of yeast tonics and similar medicaments, and for the making of those products which, spooned into mug of hot water on a cold night, give such a delicious drink.

One other aspect of beer drinking deserves honourable mention. There are all kinds of origins claimed for shandies — those drinks which are part beer and part lemonade or part beer and part ginger beer. Like other mixed drinks — such as 'mother-in-law', a nickname for a mixture of old and bitter — they undoubtedly satisfied a need for drinks pleasing to a certain taste, but also because, in the case of the shandies, they quenched a mighty thirst after a game of cricket or a day's work in the hot sun.

These shandies have their counterpart in today's scene, when the recently developed lager market in Britain has brought in its wake a liking for lager and lime. It is enough to make some traditional brewers shudder, but a man drinks his beer as he likes it and that's an end of it. In the United States incidentally, there is a sector of the beer drinking public which believes that a hangover can be averted by turning, towards the end of the evening, from lager to lager with a bottle of tomato juice added to it! From personal experience, I can tell you that this American brew is perfectly *disgusting*, but there are other beer mixtures that you might like to try even if you are not a regular beer drinker.

BEER COCKTAILS

Mild and bitter

To create a mild and bitter you don't need a half of mild and a half of bitter. You should order a pint of bitter and a half of mild, then drink the top two inches of the pint of bitter and top it up with mild. Keep topping up the bitter with the mild every two inches.

Old and mild

With this one you can actually go half and half, so simply fill a pint glass with a half pint of old, followed by a half pint of mild. The beer swilling experts maintain that putting the old in before the mild is very important, so be sure to get it right. (They are the same people who say you should always put the milk in the teacup before you pour the tea in; or is it the other way around? I never can remember.)

Old and bitter

This is the notorious 'mother-in-law' and after a few pints of it you ought to be able to face her. It is simply a half pint of old, topped up with another half pint of bitter.

Black and tan

For this one you need a half pint of stout in a pint glass, topped up with half a pint of bitter.

Lager and lime

Here it is simply a case of a pint of lager with a shot of lime-juice cordial in it.

Barley bitter

For this one you need a pint of draught bitter with a shot or maybe two of barley wine.

Black velvet

This famous concoction consists of Guinness and champagne. What proportion of champagne you top your Guinness up with depends very much on how rich you are. Personally, I wouldn't dream of ruining good champagne by mixing it with Guinness and I know an awful lot of beer drinkers who wouldn't dream of adulterating a glorious glass of Guinness with a bit of bubbly; that said, it is still a drink that one should try at least once in a lifetime.

Port and Guinness

To make this drink you must order a Guinness and a glass of port. Drink just enough of the Guinness to make room for the port and then pour the port into the Guinness. The mixture is remarkable and devastatingly intoxicating.

Rum and Guinness

To create this interesting drink, you follow exactly the same process as with the port and Guinness: order your pint of Guinness and a rum, drink enough of the Guinness to make room for the rum and then pour in the rum.

Dog's nose

This is a dangerous mixture, but very popular with would-be alcoholics. You pour a shot of gin into a pint glass and then top it up with beer.

Moscow mule

Here you put a double vodka into a half pint glass and top it up with lager. Since the vodka is almost tasteless, you'll think you are drinking a lager with an incredible kick to it, but after you've had a few you will find that not only will you not be driving home, you probably won't even be going home!

'He's champion of our darts team. Trouble is that it takes ten pints before he gets his first double.'

Spirits of the Time

THE DELICATE ART OF DISTILLATION

The origin of the art and pleasure of drinking is shrouded in the mists of time. The ancient Egyptians regarded drunkenness as a pleasantly divine sensation, and the Aztecs claimed among their ancestral gods one who was reputed to be the first drunkard! The practice of distillation is equally difficult to date and although probably discovered by some long forgotten alchemist, I like to subscribe to the ancient belief that it was a gift of the gods.

How does distillation work? Well, we start from the basic fact that water begins to boil and turn into gas at 100° C (212° F), and alcohol reaches its boiling point at the lower temperature of 78° C (172° F). Therefore if heat is applied to an alcohol-containing liquid and the temperature is kept below 100° C the alcohol alone turns into gas and separates itself from the rest. If, at the same time, an apparatus is used to collect the alcohol vapour it can be cooled down and turned back into a liquid form which will be pure alcohol. The process of distillation was described by Aristotle around 400 B.C. when he revealed how best to make sea water drinkable.

The next question which occurs is, how come there are so many different kinds of spiritous drinks? The answer is revealed by looking at the wide range of mixtures containing various flavouring elements, minerals, fruits, grains and sugar cane used in their manufacture. But even

165

though the Ancient Greeks knew about distillation they didn't know enough to create the wide range of delicious spirits we know today — from whisky to brandy.

WHISKY

The word 'whisky' comes from the Celtic term *uisgebaugh* (Scottish) or *uisgebeathe* (Irish). Both mean the same thing; 'water of life'. The English found the Celtic pronounciation too difficult so they shortened and anglicized it to 'whisky'. The world's most famous whisky is Scotch and here's how they make it.

1.   The basic product used is barley and the grain selected by the distiller must be well ripened and dry, otherwise, during storage, it could turn mouldy. Consequently, in recent years much of the grain employed has been imported from abroad.
2.   On arrival at the distillery, the barley is screened to remove any impurities or inferior grain, following which it is stored in special lofts.
3.   Next, when required, it is steeped in tanks, (called steeps) containing spring water, for a period of fifty-two to sixty-two hours.
4.   After steeping, the grain is spread out on cement floors where it is kept at a fairly constant temperature of about 15° C (59° F) until it begins to sprout, after which it is known as green malt, i.e. germinated grain. This process begins the conversion of the starch in the barley into sugar.
5.   The next stop for our friendly developing grain is at the kiln, where it is spread on a screen directly over a peat fire and it is the acrid, oily smoke swirling round and through the malt which gives Scotch whisky its distinctive flavour.
6.   After its heated encounter with the kiln, the malt is

screened again to remove its dried sprouts (which are sold for cattle food) and taken to the mill room where it is ground into meal or grist to release its sugar and other substances.

7. The next step is the mashing process where the ground malt is put into huge mash-tuns with warm water. There it soaks until the water has liquefied all the starches and they have converted into sugar. When the water has absorbed all of the goodness from the grain it is drawn off and known as wort. Here we say good-bye to the barley which may now be sold as cattle fodder. Waste not, want not!

8. The wort then passes into the fermenting vats where a small quantity of carefully nurtured pure yeast is added and fermentation takes place. It is now that the Excise Officer, together with the distiller, gauges how much spirit the wort should yield; a simple example would be say 45 litres (10 gallons) of proof spirit for every 450 litres (100 gallons) of wort.

9. When fermentation is over the resulting liquid is a rather crude kind of beer known as wash and this proceeds to the wash still, a huge copper pot with a pipe leading off the top to carry the alcohol vapour. The result of this first distillation is called low wines, which pass into another still called the spirit still from where it emerges (but only after much careful control and manipulation by the still-man) as clear, bright, new whisky.

10. Finally, our whisky is barrelled in wood with the addition of a little spring water and allowed to mature.

Although I can only describe the mere bones of the distiller's art it is important to point out that the secret of fine Scotch whisky lies in the unique skill of the blender, who examines his malt whiskies when they are about three to four years old and marries them to unmalted grain whiskies, after which they are returned to casks to honeymoon and mature further.

Straight, unblended malt whiskies are also sold in small quantities, and many pubs, to attract custom and maybe a reputation, proudly collect and display them. They cost a bit more to buy, but it's well worth trying one or two for the experience and if you can't take your spirit neat, don't, whatever you do, add anything other than a little water. Old Highland saying: there are two things that a Highlander likes naked, and one of them is malt whisky!

Irish whiskey

No, it is not made from potatoes, Irish whiskey is distilled from a fermented mash of the same grains as those used in Scotland. The 'taste' difference is due to the malt-drying kiln floor being solid, so the smoke *cannot* get at the malt, resulting in a lighter, cleaner flavour Irish whiskey is also triple-distilled and to quote a famous slogan: 'not a drop is sold, till it's seven years old'. By the way, Jameson's, well known on this side of the Irish Sea, was founded by John Jameson, ex-Sheriff Clerk of Alloa, a Scotsman born and bred!

The Irish had a legend that St Patrick taught them the art of distilling, and that it was from Ireland that the Scottish stole the art. However, it is possible that the Irish stole the art, along with St Patrick, from what was later to be known as Scotland.

American whiskies

The manufacture of American whiskies is, broadly speaking, the same as that in Scotland except, of course, that the grains are different. The whisky is placed to mature in a newly charred barrel made of white oak. The legend behind this custom of charring the barrel comes from Jamaica where a fire in a warehouse caused some barrels containing rum to be heavily charred. After a period of time it was found that the rum had acquired a colour and quality far better than usual. Another popular theory suggests that the Kentucky coopers, in order to bend more easily the staves of wood, held them over an open fire. Whether these stories are true or not matters little, but American law states that the charred barrels may only be used once and consequently they are much sought after by Scottish distillers who use them to store Scotch whisky.

Bourbon whiskey

Distilled from fermented mash of which the grain is not less than 51 % maize, it gets its name from the fact that the first whiskey distilled in Kentucky was in Georgetown, Bourbon County.

Rye whiskey

This contains not less than 51 % rye grain and together with Bourbon is designated 'straight whiskey'.

Canadian whisky

There are those who believe that Canadian whisky is rye whisky. In fact, it is made from a mixture of rye, corn, wheat and barley malt, the exact proportions of each being a trade secret of the individual distiller. Note here that in Ireland and America the product is spelled with an 'e' while in Scotland and Canada they manage without. Japan, Holland, Germany, Denmark and Australia also produce their own whiskies. Try them if you care to. On the whole, I don't.

GIN

This spirit, without which the dry martini cocktail would be a very tame affair, was invented in the seventeenth century by one Franciscus de la Boe, a physician and professor at Holland's University of Leyden. He was known also as Dr Sylvius and the intention of his creation was purely medicinal. Aware of the diuretic properties of the oil of the juniper berry, he thought that by redistilling a pure alcohol with the berry he could obtain its therapeutic oil in a form which would provide an inexpensive medicine. He was right, and, in a few short years the entire population of the country found itself stricken by ills which could only be cured by Dr Sylvius' magical medicine! He named it *genièvre*, after the French name for the juniper berry. The Dutch called it *genever* and the English shortened it to gin. English soldiers returning from the seventeenth century wars on the Continent brought home a taste for this 'Dutch courage' as they called it, and, in a very little time, gin became the national drink of the country. (Scotch, incidentally, has only been truly popular in England for about a century).

Queen Anne assisted the gin industry greatly by raising the taxes on French wines and brandies and lowering those on English distilled spirits. Gin was very cheap as can be seen from this sign erected by one innkeeper of the time:

'Drunk for a penny,
Dead drunk for twopence,
Clean straw for nothing.'

Gin is made from grain mixture and following the first distillation the spirit is reduced to the correct strength by adding distilled water. It is then distilled again in the company of its flavouring agents, the principal one of these belonging to the juniper berry. Other ingredients vary from company to company and their formula is a closely guarded secret, creating as it does the distinctive character of individual brands. Some of these flavouring materials, known as 'botanicals' include dried lemon and

170

orange peel, coriander seed, licorice, caraway and, among many more, orris root.

Finally, the gin is reduced again to bottling strength and if not bottled straight away is stored in steel or glass lined tanks, since gin is not usually 'aged'.

There are only two main types of gin: Dutch and dry.

Dutch gin: Hollands, Genever or Schiedam gin.

Dry gin: English or American gin. (Dutch gin shouldn't be used for making cocktails because its own very distinctive taste can overshadow the other ingredients.)

London dry gin: So called because at one time most English gin was made in or around London, but the term has since been adopted by several other countries including America.

Plymouth gin: A 'heavier', more strongly flavoured gin than the 'London' type and considered by many the correct spirit to use for 'pink gin', i.e. angostura bitters and gin mixed with water to taste.

Old Tom Gin: A sweetened gin and a rare commodity nowadays. Its title is accredited to one Captain Dudley Bradstreet, a former government spy who rented a house in London, nailed the sign of a cat to the ground-floor window and put a lead pipe under its paw. Passers-by were invited to put their money into the cat's mouth and whisper, 'Puss give me 2d worth of gin,' whereupon the liquor came pouring out of the tube! This was perhaps the world's first vending machine.

Sloe gin: A liqueur, about 47° proof and made by steeping ripe sloe berries in gin.

VODKA

The word means 'little-water' and it is distilled from fermented grain mash at very high proof. Nothing is added to the neutral spirit which leaves the finished product odourless, tasteless and colourless. A special feature of its manufacture is the use of vegetable charcoal to purify it, although other government approved means can be employed.

Vodka was first produced in Russia in the fourteenth century but remained unknown outside the Baltic states and Poland until the middle of the twentieth century. It was produced in America after the repeal of Prohibition in 1933 but had to wait for fame until 1948 when a Hollywood restaurant owner found himself with a large stock of ginger beer on his hands. To avoid taking a loss on this commodity he mixed it with vodka, added half a lime, served it in a copper mug and named it 'Moscow Mule'. The drink caught on and swept the country. Due to its lack of taste and smell it has the convenient social quality of leaving its imbiber, in the best sense of the word, breathless. In the cocktail world vodka is recognized as the most versatile of mixers since it can be blended with any beverage and may be 'felt but not smelt'.

RUM

The first and most surprising fact about rum is that it comes from grass. The botanical name for the particular grass concerned is of little interest (i.e. I can't remember it), but I am familiar with its common name: sugar cane. Columbus took sugar cane from the Canary Islands to the West Indies where it prospered and made sugar no longer an expensive luxury. The early Spanish settlers in the West Indies noticed that the residual molasses of their sugar factories fermented easily and they began to distil from it. The result was found to be delightful, and the freebooters had no problem in selling it to Europe where the new concoction was warmly welcomed.

How it got its name is uncertain: some believe that it was a contraction of the Latin *saccharum*, meaning sugar, and others credit the name to the English navy. In 1745 Admiral Vernon discovered that his men were suffering from scurvy. He gave them this new beverage, which cured their problem and earned him their gratitude and the title 'Old Rummy'. The term 'rum' at that time meant anything or anyone of the best and finest quality, so when these happy sailors named the drink 'rum' it was the highest accolade they could bestow.

The making of rum begins with the harvesting of the sugar cane which is taken to the sugar mills and crushed to remove the juice. The juice is then boiled to concentrate the sugar and to remove the water. The resulting sugar syrup is put into vast drums and spun rapidly to extract the heavy, thick substance called molasses. After further treatment the molasses is mixed with water and yeast containing slops from a previous production. This 'wash' is then distilled after fermentation, and the result is rum.

There are many different kinds of rum depending on where it is made, the yeasts employed, and the amount of caramel used for colouring. Rum, like whisky, needs to mature and in this country cannot be sold when it is less than three years old.

BRANDY

Brandy is a drinkable spirit obtained by distilling wine or fermented grape juice. It can be made in almost any country in the world, but the finest of them all is French Cognac brandy, closely followed by its national sister, Armagnac.

The art of distillation, although an ancient one, wasn't

applied to wine until the sixteenth century when the brandy trade began. According to legend, at that time there was a healthy trade in wine between La Rochelle on the west coast of France and Holland, but as there was great risk at sea, in order to save valuable shipping space an enterprising young Dutch shipper hit upon the idea of distilling his wine with the intention of adding water to it on its safe arrival in port. Upon tasting this 'soul' of the wine his Dutch associates liked it so much that they decided it would be a waste of water to dilute so delightful a spirit — which is how and why the brandy trade began.

The Dutch named the new product *brandewijn* (burnt wine) because the heat was the prime agent in its manufacture and it is from this Dutch word that we get the name brandy.

Cognac

The unique qualities of cognac responsible for its great reputation include the special centuries-old method of distillation together with an ideal combination of chalky soil and charming climate. Surprisingly, the wine used to make this world-famous drink is unremarkable and the great cognac houses buy their stocks from small farmers (numbering some 70,000) who grow their own white grapes within the carefully defined area of Cognac. For every ten barrels of wine used the yield is one barrel of brandy, and, as it comes colourless from the copper still, it is barrelled in oak casks and laid away in dark cellars to age. Due to evaporation through the pores in the wood as much cognac is lost into the air each year as is drunk in the whole of France!

Two years is the minimum time allowed by law for ageing and during this process the brandy gradually takes on a lovely amber tone with the delicate natural bouquet of grape blossom. Precise blending in vast oaken vats with rotating paddles is essential before bottling, and each 'house' has its own secret formula which includes reducing to shipping strength by adding distilled water and the use of caramel to maintain a uniform colour.

What about all those stars and letters on brandy bottles? They refer not to age, but to quality, and even that definition varies from house to house. The 'star' system has an interesting history; superstition abounds among wine people, including the firm belief that comet years produce fine wines. Thus, the legend goes, in the comet year of 1811, a superb brandy was produced and one of the shippers designated the brandy of that year with a star. The following year's brandy was equally fine and to this he granted two stars. By now he had caught the habit but fortunately ceased the practice when he reached five stars. Actually, the famous house of Hennessy claims to have begun the star system. And while I'm on the subject of famous names, you'll be amused to know that three of the most illustrious are not from France at all: Richard Hennessy came from Ireland, Mr Martell came from the Channel Islands and Mr Hine from Dorset!

Apart from the 'star' system there are also those assorted combinations of letters such as V.S.O.P., X.O., V.V.O., etc. Oddly, they represent, not French but English words:

V	–	Very	E	–	Especial
S	–	Superior	X	–	Extra
O	–	Old	F	–	Fine
P	–	Pale	C	–	Cognac

To answer the question, 'What is the best age for cognac?' let me quote a gentleman of the region; 'Cognac is like a woman. She is at her best between the ages of twenty-five and forty.' No doubt armed with this knowledge he had a full and happy life.

Armagnac

Second only to cognac this other great brandy is quite different in style due to the soil of its region, its more southerly geographical location, the 'black oak' casks in which it is matured and a different distilling process which enables the spirit to begin its life with a stronger flavour and scent. Its drier taste and pungent aroma linger in the mouth with intensely pleasurable effect.

'Modest, George is not.'

Cocktail Cavalcade

THE ORIGINAL COCKTAIL

I am very keen on cocktails and I am delighted to see that they have been making something of a come-back recently. Gin and tonic and whisky and water are all very well, but they get terribly boring after a while. Cocktails are much more fun to drink and much more fun to prepare. Obviously, they do require rather more effort, but the effort is well rewarded and I firmly believe that anyone who knows how to create a perfect cocktail has managed to master one of the world's great art forms.

Cocktails, of course, are an American invention. When you go to the United States the food is disgusting and the wine indifferent, but you tend to get wonderfully good cocktails in advance of the food, in fact they are so splendid that you don't really taste the food when it arrives and so powerful that you don't really miss the wine! The Americans have a number of entertaining stories of the origin of the term 'cocktail' meaning mixed drink. The most respectable — and the one most generally excepted as authentic — dates back 200 years.

Back in 1779 there was a lively tavern in the town of Yorktown, Virginia, run by an Irish lady called Betsy Flanagan. The tavern was a popular meeting place for the officers of Washington's army. Adjoining the tavern was a large chicken farm owned by a pro-British Tory and both the Tory and his chickens were the subject of much banter from the soldiers. One day, Betsy decided to make the

'We're very proud of Father. He once gave his name to a cocktail.'

cocky warriors eat their own words. This she did by holding a Tory chicken party, and once the feast was over, inviting the officers into the bar where she provided a plentiful suppy of an eighteenth-century concoction called a bracer. The bracers were in bottles and every single bottle was adorned with a cock's tail feather. There was a French officer present and he proposed the toast, 'Vive le cocktail', and from that day onwards Betsy's bracers were known as cocktails.

Another diverting explanation for the origin of the word 'cocktail' comes from the old-time Mississippi river steamers, where a well-heeled traveller would occasionally call for a tub to be filled with every available liquor on board. The glasses used to contain this vile mixture, were, by tradition, shaped in the form of a cock's breast and to stir the concoction a rod formed like a cock's tail was used.

While the Americans may claim to have invented the cocktail, there can be no doubt that in the year A.D. 200 the Emperor Commodius was regularly drinking a tasty little tipple composed of lemon juice and powdered adders, and classical scholars are inclined to claim that this was, in fact, the very first cocktail. (In less lucid moments, I have sometimes wondered whether there was any connection between this drink and that well-known Australian expression 'going for a snakes'?)

Whatever the true explanation for the origin of the cocktail, the fact remains that it is still with us, and growing new feathers every year.

COCKTAILS AT HOME – or Granny can never find her glasses, (she just puts them down when she empties them)

I am about to introduce you to fifty or so of my favourite cocktails. As you will see from the recipes the range of drinks used in creating cocktails can, at first sight, seem

'Remember, Charles, it doesn't taste the same unless you achieve a regular three to the bar.'

dauntingly wide. However, it is possible to acquire a stock of well-known basic ingredients, which on their own are sufficiently popular to ensure that you won't be left with the dust gathering on an accumulation of obscure bottles.

Here is a list of everyday drinks which form the basis of a large number of the most delightful cocktails: Scotch whisky, gin, vodka, brandy, rum, sherry, vermouth (sweet and dry), Dubonnet, wine (red and white), beer, orange and lemon squash, lime juice, tomato, orange and pineapple juice, lemonade, soda water, tonic water, bitter lemon, dry ginger, cola, mineral water, angostura bitters, Worcestershire sauce, sugar syrup.

(Sugar syrup can be made by boiling together one cup of sugar and one cup of water. When the sugar is dissolved allow the syrup to cool, bottle it and it will keep in the fridge for a long time.)

You will also need glasses, and, for most cocktails, a 2 or 3 oz size is ideal. Other essential bits of equipment include a strainer, to hold back the ice, a mixing glass (for which a straight-sided pint glass or jug will suit), a mixing spoon, a shaker (for which a screw top jar can be substituted) and, of course, a good supply of ice. (If you are having a party, the best place to keep ice is in the washing machine because as it melts there is no mess to worry about!)

Other extras you may need, depending on the recipe, include oranges, lemons, cucumbers, cherries, tiny pickled onions, a cloth for mopping up and a clean glass cloth to add that polished sparkle to your cocktail glasses.

The two basic ways of making a cocktail are *mixing* and *shaking* and the relevant instruction is given at the end of each recipe. This is how it's done:

To mix Put ice into the mixing glass, add the prescribed ingredients, stir vigorously until chilled and then strain into the serving glasses.

To shake Put ice into the cocktail shaker, add the prescribed ingredients, put the top back on the shaker, shake for a short time with even more vigour and strain into the required glasses.

COCKTAIL RECIPES

The amounts given in these recipes are all in proportion and I am going to begin with the most popular and widely drunk cocktail in the world, the Dry Martini, which through the years has become progressively dryer. Originally called the Martinez Cocktail when invented by Professor Jerry Thomas in the mid-nineteenth century, by 1933 it was simply known as a Martini and the standard recipe was four parts of dry gin to one part of dry vermouth with a twist of lemon peel. Then came the Second World War and the 'tomorrow we die' psychology provided the excuse for the fifteen to one Martini! Here is the standard recipe for today which can also be had 'on the rocks'. (Before adding the strip of lemon peel twist it over the drink to release the zest.)

Dry Martini

¾ dry gin   ¼ dry vermouth

Mix, add a twist of lemon peel, or an olive on a cocktail stick. The use of a small pickled onion instead of lemon or an olive creates a Gibson which dates back to the beginning of the twentieth century when a bartender at the New York Players Club was mixing a Martini for the artist Charles Dana Gibson. The barman discovered there were no more olives, substituted a pearl onion and named the drink after his customer.

Alexander

A personal favourite this, named for Alexander the Great, centuries after his death, and also the first drink given to Lee Remick by Jack Lemmon in the famous film *Days of Wine and Roses*.

⅓ crème de cacao   ⅓ brandy

⅓ fresh cream

Shake

Adonis

('He seems a nice boy')

⅓ sweet vermouth   dash orange bitters

⅔ dry sherry   twist orange peel

Mix

Affinity

⅔ Scotch whisky   2 dashes angostura bitters

⅓ sweet vermouth

Mix

COCKTAILS FOR LOVERS

Cupid's Bow

¼ gin   ¼ aurum (or curaçao)

¼ Forbidden Fruit liqueur   ¼ passion fruit juice

Shake

Fallen Angel

¾ gin

¼ fresh lemon or lime juice

Shake

2 dashes crême de menthe

1 dash angostura bitters

Bosom Caresser

⅔ brandy

⅓ orange curacao

Shake (4 oz glass)

1 yoke of egg

1 teaspoon sugar syrup

Between the sheets

⅓ brandy

⅓ white rum

Shake

⅓ cointreau

1 dash of lemon juice

First night

½ brandy

¼ Van der Hum

Shake

¼ Tia Maria

1 teaspoon cream

Roberta May

(on the other hand she may not!)

⅓ vodka

⅓ aurum

Shake

⅓ orange squash

½ teaspoon egg white

Honeymoon

⅓ Benedictine

⅓ calvados

Shake

⅓ lemon juice

3 dashes of orange curaçao

Playmate

¼ brandy

¼ apricot brandy

¼ Grand Marnier

¼ orange squash

Shake

white of egg

dash of angostura

twist of orange peel

Témptation

⁷⁄₁₀ rye whisky

¹⁄₁₀ orange curaçao

¹⁄₁₀ Pernod

Shake

¹⁄₁₀ Dubonnet

twist orange peel

twist lemon peel

Maiden's Prayer

(Which calls to mind the Irish maiden's prayer, 'Lord have Murphy on me!')

⅜ gin

⅜ cointreau

⅛ orange juice

⅛ lemon juice

Shake

Nimmo's Knockout

¼ brandy

¼ Pernod

Shake

¼ dry vermouth

¼ curaçao

Sweet Memories

(Perhaps for the older man with a reminder from writer Upton Sinclair; 'Cocktail's may help one regain the feeling, but not the fact.')

⅓ bacardi rum

⅓ orange curaçao

⅓ dry vermouth

Mix

COCKTAILS WITH A TOUCH OF CLASS

Claridge

⅓ gin

⅙ cointreau

⅓ dry vermouth

⅙ apricot brandy

Mix

Coronation

½ sherry

1 dash marashino

½ dry vermouth

2 dashes orange bitters

Mix

Dubonnet Royal

⅔ Dubonnet

2 dashes orange curaçao

⅓ gin

1 dash Pernod

2 dashes angostura

Mix and add a cherry.

Duchess

⅓ sweet vermouth ⅓ Pernod
⅓ dry vermouth

Mix

Duke

½ Drambuie ¼ lemon juice
¼ orange juice 1 egg

Shake, and serve in a wine glass with a splash of champagne on top.

Embassy Royal

½ bourbon ¼ sweet Martini
¼ Drambuie 2 dashes of orange squash

Shake

Empire Glory

(A classic cocktail from the days when girls still had hidden charms.)

½ rye ¼ lemon juice
¼ ginger wine 2 dashes of sugar syrup

Shake

Guards

⅔ gin 3 dashes of orange curaçao
⅓ sweet vermouth

Mix

Little Princess
½ white rum   ½ sweet vermouth
Mix

Princess Mary
⅓ gin   ⅓ fresh cream
⅓ crème de cacao
Shake

Royal Romance
½ gin   ¼ dry passion fruit juice
¼ Grand Marnier   1 dash sugar syrup
Shake

Royal Smile
⅔ gin   3 dashes sugar syrup
⅓ calvados   3 dashes lemon juice
Shake

COCKTAILS FOR THE MAN IN A MILLION

Millionaire No. 1
⅟₁₀ brandy   ⅟₁₀ orgeat syrup
⅟₁₀ crème de noyau   2 dashes angostura
⅟₁₀ orange curaçao
Shake

188

Millionaire No. 2

⅔ rye

⅓ grenadine

white of egg

2 dashes orange curaçao

dash of Pernod

Shake (large glass)

(And talking of millionaires, I once knew a man who had a 20-metre swimming pool filled with Scotch whisky. When you went down for the third time you had a smile on your face!)

COCKTAILS TO COPE WITH COMPREHENSIVE EDUCATION

Old Etonian

½ gin

½ Lillet

2 dashes orange bitters

2 dashes crême de noyeau

twist of orange peel

Mix

Harvard

½ brandy

½ sweet vermouth

2 dashes angostura

1 dash sugar syrup

twist of lemon

Mix

COCKTAILS TO REVIVE THE TIRED MOTORIST

Bentley

½ Dubonnet

½ calvados

Mix

R.A.C.

½ gin

dash orange bitters

¼ dry vermouth

1 cherry and twist of orange

dash grenadine

Mix

Sidecar

½ brandy

¼ lemon juice

¼ cointreau

Shake

THE COCKTAIL MAKER'S ALPHABET

A.I.

⅓ Grand Marnier

dash grenadine

⅔ gin

twist lemon peel

dash lemon juice

Shake

Bronx

(This drink was named in 1919 after the New York City borough which, in turn, is named after Jonas Bronck, a Dane who first settled the area for the Dutch West India Company in 1641.)

½ gin

⅙ dry vermouth

⅙ sweet vermouth

⅙ fresh orange juice

Shake

'*Drink up, sir. The cherry dissolves in fifty seconds.*'

Commodore

⁴/₅ rye
¹/₅ fresh lime juice
2 dashes orange bitters
castor sugar to taste

Shake

Dandy

½ rye
½ Dubonnet
dash angostura
3 dashes cointreau
twist orange and lemon peel

Mix

Evans

(Despite the name rather rare in the Rhonda)

⁴/₅ rye
¹/₁₀ apricot brandy
¹/₁₀ orange curaçao

Mix

Fourth Degree

⅓ gin
⅓ dry vermouth
⅓ sweet vermouth
2 dashes Pernod

Mix

Gimlet

(British naval surgeon Sir T. O. Gimlette believed that straight gin harmed the health of naval officers and created the 'healthy cocktail' by diluting gin with lime juice in 1890.)

⅔ gin
⅓ lime juice cordial

Mix

Harvey Wallbanger

(Very popular today and named after the Californian surfer, Tom Harvey, whose favourite drink was a 'Screwdriver' — ⅓ vodka, ⅔ orange juice, combined with a few drops of the Italian liqueur Galliano. Having concluded a day's surfing Harvey would visit his local bar carrying his surfboard, which used to bang against the wall.)

⅓ vodka   ⅔ orange juice

Shake. Strain into a tall glass filled with ice, float two teaspoons of Galliano on top and serve with straws.

Inspiration

¼ gin   ¼ calvados
¼ dry vermouth   ¼ Grand Marnier

Mix. Add a cherry.

Jack-In-The-Box

½ calvados   dash angostura
½ pineapple juice

Shake

Kelvin 66

¼ aquavit   ¼ Dubonnet
¼ Grand Marnier   ¼ orange squash

Shake. Add a cherry.

Linstead

½ Scotch whisky

dash Pernod

½ sweet pineapple juice

twist lemon peel

Shake

Manhattan

(This concoction is named after the Manhattan Club in New York where it was first mixed in the mid 1870s at a dinner given by Lady Randolph Churchill in honour of Governor Samuel J. Tilden. The club got its name from the Manhatten Indians who sold the island to the Dutch for trinkets worth 24 dollars!)

⅔ rye

dash angostura

⅓ sweet vermouth

Mix. Add a cherry.

Negroni

⅓ gin

⅓ Campari

⅓ sweet vermouth

On the rocks (i.e. ice), ½ slice of orange, soda if required.

Mix

Old Fashioned

(Use 6 oz whisky glass)

rye or bourbon

lump of sugar plus enough water to dissolve it

3 dashes angostura

ice, ½ slice orange, cherry, stirring rod or short straws.

Mix

Piccadilly

⅔ gin   dash Pernod
⅓ dry vermouth   dash grenadine

Mix

Quarter Deck

⅔ dark rum   dash lime juice cordial
⅓ dry sherry

Mix

Rob Roy

(The nickname of the legendary eighteenth-century freebooter, Robert Macgregor).

½ Scotch whisky   dash angostura
½ sweet vermouth

Mix. Add a cherry.

Shamrock

(Known to some as the Irish diamond: sham-rock).

½ Irish whiskey   3 dashes green charteuse
½ dry vermouth   3 dashes green crème de
                         menthe
Mix

Tango

½ gin   2 dashes orange curaçao
¼ sweet vermouth   dash orange juice
¼ dry vermouth

Shake

Up-to-date

⅖ rye   .   ⅕ Grand Marnier
⅖ dry vermouth   dash angostura
Mix. Add a twist of lemon peel.

Vodkatini

⅔ vodka   ⅓ dry vermouth
Mix. Add a twist of lemon peel.

White Lady

½ gin   ¼ Cointreau
¼ lemon juice   dash egg white
Shake

Yellow Daisy

⅖ gin   ⅕ Grand Marnier
⅖ dry vermouth
Mix

Xanthia

⅓ gin   ⅓ cherry brandy
⅓ yellow chartreuse
Mix

Zaza

½ gin   dash angostura
½ Dubonnet
Mix

THE GLOBE TROTTER'S COCKTAIL COMPENDIUM

Alaska

One of the United States since 1959. Originally settled by the Russians in the eighteenth century. Famous for its gold strikes in 1899 and 1902, Alaska now produces fish, fur, timber, minerals and oil. Population: 302,000.

¾ gin   ¼ Yellow Chartreuse

Shake

Bermudiana Rose

The island of Bermuda, settled by the English in 1609, relies for its up-keep on well-heeled tourists. Population: 54,000. If you can't find Rose, there are lots of other lovely girls!

⅖ gin   ⅕ grenadine

⅕ apricot brandy   ⅕ lemon juice

Shake

Bombay

Major port and industrial centre of West India. Population of greater city: 5,969,000.

½ brandy   dash Pernod

¼ dry vermouth   2 dashes orange curaçao

¼ sweet vermouth

Mix

Brazil

The exotic republic of East South America, famous for its coffee. The population speaks Portuguese (since the sixteenth century) and numbers 95,408,000.

½ dry sherry

½ dry vermouth

dash angostura

dash Pernod

twist lemon peel

Mix

Havana

The capital of Cuba, famous for its cigars. Fidel Castro lives here. Population: 1,755,000.

½ apricot brandy

¼ gin

¼ Swedish punch

dash lemon juice

Shake

Hawaiian

Hawaii, the fiftieth state of the U.S.A. and one of a group of islands discovered by Captain Cook in 1778, after which they were called the Sandwich Islands because the fourth Earl of Sandwich was First Lord of the Admiralty at the time. Population: 770,000.

½ gin

½ orange juice

dash orange curaçao

Shake

Jamaica Joe

Discovered by Columbus in 1494. Captured by England from Spain 1655. Exports include fruit, spices, tobacco and sugar. Population: 1,897,000.

1/3 rum   1/3 advocaat

1/3 Tia Maria

Shake. Add a dash of grenadine and a little grated nutmeg on top.

San Francisco

Well known for its Golden Gate Bridge, Chinatown, tram cars, hippies and hills. Population: 704,000.

1/3 gin   dash orange bitters

1/3 dry vermouth   dash angostura

1/3 sweet vermouth

Mix. Add a cherry.

COCKTAIL SPECIALS

Heading the list is the greatest party 'ice breaker' of all time.

Champagne Cocktail

Saturate a lump of sugar with angostura in a champagne or wine glass.
Add half a measure of brandy.
Top up with chilled champagne.
Add a slice of orange.

If funds are limited one can substitute a dry (brut) vin mousseux for the real thing. It won't taste *quite* the same, but the effect is just as good.

An invaluable 'trick of the trade' was passed on to me by a cocktail barman I met many years ago, in Blackheath of all places. He showed me how to prepare a 'mock champagne cocktail': follow the directions as before but instead of champagne use a measure of pale dry sherry and top up with soda water!

Another money saving tip when serving champagne is to have the bottles very well iced. This will impair the taste of the wine, but because it is so very cold people won't drink it too quickly. The most efficient method for chilling a number of bottles of champagne, or indeed any white wine, is to lay them in the bath covered with cold water and lots of ice. The mixture of ice and water will do the cooling job in about half the time of ice alone.

Bucks Fizz

½ chilled fresh orange juice   ½ chilled champagne

Black Velvet

½ chilled Guiness   ½ chilled champagne

Both these drinks should ideally be served in half pint tankards.

Cobblers ('I beg your pardon')

From America and very popular in warm climates. Wine or spirits can be used for the base.

Fill medium-sized wine glass with ice.

Pour over chosen base   1 teaspoon of castor sugar

4 dashes orange curaçao

Stir

Decorate with fruit and sprig of mint if liked and serve with straws.
(Conventional sized straws can be cut down to required size with a clean razor blade or very sharp knife.)

Collins

John Collins was the head waiter at Limmer's in Hanover Square in the nineteenth century and although this concoction bears his name, it very closely resembles the equally famous 'Gin Sling'. Pimm's claim that their No. 1 is the original.

Fill a tall glass (highball) with ice

Add juice of 1 lemon

1 teaspoon of castor sugar

Measure of gin

Top up with soda water

Stir, and serve with slice of lemon

Go to work on an egg nog

The most enterprising egg salesman of all time must surely be Thomas Lipton who, at the age of fourteen, advised his father that his mother should serve the eggs since her hands being smaller made the eggs look bigger!

Basic egg nog

1 egg	1 measure brandy
1 tablespoon of castor sugar	1 measure dark rum

Shake, and strain into a goblet.
Add milk and a little grated nutmeg.

Breakfast egg nog

1 egg   1 measure brandy
1 measure of orange curaçao Add milk

Shake, and strain into a goblet with little grated nutmeg on top. Hot milk may be used if desired.

FIZZES

Gin Fizz

Measure gin   teaspoon of castor sugar
juice of 1 lemon

Shake, and strain, top up with soda water.

Merry Widow Fizz

1 measure lemon juice   double measure Dubonnet
1 measure orange juice   white of egg

Shake, and strain, top up with soda water.

Pineapple Fizz

large measure pineapple juice 1 teaspoon of castor sugar
large measure white rum

Shake, and strain, top up with ½ soda and ½ lemonade.

FLIPS

This is a range of drinks which were highly popular in the nineteenth century, the mixture being heated and stirred with a hot iron known as a flip-iron. Nowadays they are usually taken cold.

Boston Flip

½ rye

½ Madeira

Shake, and strain.

yolk of egg

1 teaspoon castor sugar

Sifi Flip

½ gin

¼ cointreau

¼ grenadine

Shake, and strain.

juice ½ a lemon

yolk of egg

Night Cap Flip

⅓ anisette

⅓ orange curaçao

Shake, and strain.

⅓ brandy

yolk of egg

FRAPPÉS

To prepare a frappé you require a medium-sized glass with a stem, filled to the brim with crushed ice. (A useful method for crushing ice is to wrap the required number of ice cubes in a strong tea towel or cloth and pound them with a rolling pin or other handy-sized unbreakable instrument.) Any favourite liqueur may be used — crême de menthe is the most popular — and the drink is served with short straws. Overleaf are two recipes for frappé cocktails featuring more than one liqueur.

THE NAP FRAPPÉ

$1/_3$ kummel $1/_3$ brandy
$1/_3$ green chartreuse

Ward's Frappé

rind of lemon in the glass   ½ brandy
½ green chartreuse

NB: do *not* mix, and add the ingredients in the order given.

HIGHBALLS

Vulgar jokes apart, this concoction from nineteenth-century America orginated with the U.S. railroad companies' practice of placing a ball on top of a high pole to indicate to a passing train driver that he was behind time and should increase his speed. What our brothers in A.S.L.E.F. would think of this I really don't care to guess but the term 'highball' has now come to mean a quickly prepared, simple drink.

Any preferred spirit may be used, and it is put into a tall glass filled with ice. Top up with dry ginger ale or soda water adding a twist of lemon rind. My favourite member of the highball family is the Horse's Neck.

Horse's Neck

Peel the rind off a lemon in one continuous spiral. Curl one end of the lemon over the edge of the glass with the ice holding the rest in place.

Add a measure of brandy.

Top up with dry ginger.

Add a dash of angostura if desired.

The Mint Julep

First described in print by Captain Marryatt in 1815 after he had been introduced to the drink by a wealthy planter in the Southern States of America. Here is the present-day recipe.

Into a tall glass place the following:

6 sprigs fresh mint

1 tablespoon castor sugar

1 tablespoon water

Crush together until the sugar is dissolved.

Add 1 measure of bourbon and fill the glass with crushed ice. Stir until the outside of the glass has become frosted. Serve with straws and a sprig of mint on top.

PUNCH

The name 'punch' is derived from an old Hindi word meaning 'five'. The basic ingredients of early recipes were: (1) spirit; (2) water; (3) sugar; (4) lemon and (5) spice. The drink has often been described as a self-contradiction in that the spirit makes it strong, the water makes it weak, the sugar makes it sweet and the lemon makes it sour. According to Mrs Beeton's *Book of Household Management* (1861), it was very popular with the middle classes at the beginning of the nineteenth century until it was eventually superseded by wine.

Planter's Punch

Tall glass half-filled with ice 1 teaspoon grenadine

1 dash angostura   1 measure dark rum

fresh lemon or lime juice

Add soda water and *stir,* with slices of orange and lemon on top.

Brandy Punch

Large wine or whisky glass   crushed ice
measure brandy   dry ginger ale
4 dashes curaçao
Stir, add sprig of mint and slice of orange.

Claret Punch

Large wine or whisky glass   2 dashes orange curaçao
measure claret   1 teaspoon castor sugar
lemon juice
Stir, add ice and slices of orange and lemon. Top up with
dry ginger ale.

SOME LIKE IT HOT

'Grog'

'Grog' is an old naval term applied first as a nickname to
Admiral Vernon who wore a grogram cloak. Later, when
he ordered that water should be added to the crew's ration
of neat spirit, this mixture was accorded the title.

Large strong glass   lemon juice
measure dark rum   small stick cinnamon
1 lump sugar   fill with boiling water and *stir*
2 cloves

NB: To prevent a glass from cracking, place a metal spoon
inside before adding the boiling water.

Hot Buttered Rum (highly recommended if you have a cold).

Large strong glass	a slice of butter
1 measure dark rum	4 cloves
1 lump sugar	

Fill with boiling water and *stir* until the butter has melted.

Irish Coffee

A justly famous drink and here, after much careful research, is *the* Irish Coffee story:

In the early 1940s there was a flying-boat base at Foynes in County Clare. This was in the days when the Clippers — which were giant sea-planes — flew between Europe and America, and Foynes was the last refuelling stop before the long western transatlantic crossing and it was also, of course, the first point in Europe at which they touched down when coming east. The chief chef at Foynes, in those times, was a man called Joe Sheridan and one day he had to cope with a load of very tired, dispirited and delayed passengers who, as P. G. Wodehouse might well have said had he been there, were far from gruntled.

Joe — being the nice man he was — wondered what special something he could give them to cheer their hearts. Many people, when they are cold, drink hot coffee — and equally many people when they are tired drink Irish whisky. Why not, he thought, combine both cold Irish whisky and very hot coffee? So he took a glass and poured in a generous amount of Irish whisky and then filled it to about three-quarters of an inch from the brim with very hot black coffee. He then added sugar and stirred. The result was delightful, but he felt something was missing. It needed some other ingredient to give it a special distinctive flavour uniquely its own. He wondered what would happen if he were to pour milk on it and, of course, the inevitable did happen and the milk sank, as did some cream he used later, and the mixtures looked a sort of brownish-beige which was far from attractive. Then he thought, if one were to whip the cream slightly and pour it so that it fell gently on the surface of the coffee it might stay there. Well, as we all know, it did.

From the moment he first served it, Irish Coffee was an immediate success and its fame soon spread throughout the world. The owner of the famous Buena Vista restaurant in San Francisco, for example, tasted it on her way through Shannon Airport (which replaced Foynes) and she did not rest until she had persuaded Joe Sheridan to come to San Francisco and help her to promote its sale. (She also founded the Irish Coffee Group of America whose membership includes some of the world's best-known names).

The Buena Vista continues to serve thousands of Irish Coffees each year and no one who visits that restaurant would dream of leaving without finishing their meal with Joe Sheridan's marvellous drink.

WHAT ABOUT MY DRINK, DADDY?

There are a number of cocktails suitable for children, teetotallers, light-headed lady drivers and the like, the most famous being:

The Pussyfoot

⅓ fresh orange juice	dash grenadine
⅓ fresh lemon juice	yolk of egg
⅓ lime juice	

Shake well

Parson's Special

4 dashes grenadine   yolk of egg

56 ml (2 oz) orange juice

Shake, and strain into a medium-sized glass with a dash of soda on top.

Cinderella

As the ugly sisters exclaimed when the invitation arrived at Hardup Hall, 'No balls for Cinderella unti she's twenty-one!' However, this little concoction deserves the personal approval of anybody's fairy godmother.

⅓ lemon juice   ⅓ pineapple juice

⅓ orange juice

Shake, and strain into medium-sized glass.

And to conclude this innocuous thirst-quenching quartet, an item named after Snow White's favourite colour and size of person:

Yellow Dwarf

1 yolk of egg   ½ almond syrup

½ cream

Shake, strain and top up with dash of soda water.

Footnote: I can't end a chapter on cocktails and mixed drinks without giving a mention to that notorious gentleman, Mickey Finn. It seems that this was the name of a bartender working in Chicago around the turn of the century who served knockout drinks to unsuspecting customers in order to rob them. Nowadays, in all too many bars, this is achieved with the victim fully conscious!

The Hangover Report

WHAT IS A HANGOVER?

You know the symptoms, of course — the headache, the distressed feeling in the abdomen, the flashing spots before the eyes, the aches in places which you'd never noticed *existed* before. . . . Well, these symptoms have a variety of causes.

Some are caused by the alcohol *itself*. In particular, alcohol is quite a strong *irritant* of the stomach — which is why too much of it makes certain people rather unpleasantly sick. And after a night of sampling the grape or the grain (or both) most of us feel the results of that gastric irritation — in other words, discomfort in the tummy, plus a marked aversion to food.

And some hangover symptoms are caused by something called *acetaldehyde*. This is the stuff into which alcohol is broken down in the body, and it circulates in your bloodstream in quite hefty quantities on the morning after the night before. Since this is one of a group of chemicals used as powerful disinfectants, you can understand why your poor, fragile body feels more than a little toxic on such occasions.

Thirdly, a very important cause of the 'hangover syndrome' is a group of chemicals called *congeners*. Never heard of them? Well, the congeners are the things that are largely responsible for giving alcoholic drinks their flavour. In general, 'rich' drinks are high in congeners, and drinks with relatively little taste are low in them. (There are exceptions, but let it pass.) Congeners are quite nice, jolly sorts of chemicals (they even *sound* congenial, don't they), provided you have a moderate amount of them, but if you have too much, they play merry hell with your system.

There are two other factors which tend to make a hangover worse. The first is *lack of sleep*. People often forget that after going to an all-night rave-up they're decidedly shorter of sleep than usual. For some of us, this doesn't matter very much — but for others, the lack of sleep plays a considerable part in exacerbating the hangover.

The other factor is an old-fashioned thing called *guilt*. If someone goes on a real bender, then some at least of his misery the next day will usually be caused by a certain sense of remorse at overdoing things. If you've merely had two drinks more than you should, this remorse may not be very great. On the other hand, if in the middle of the party you insulted your boss, picked a fight with the local magistrate, indecently assaulted the vicar's wife, and professed undying love for your bank manager's mistress, it is just possible that a certain vague sense of guilt may be making the *teeniest* contribution to your hangover.

PREVENTING HANGOVERS

Here are six basic rules for preventing hangovers:
1. Avoid excessive drinking!
2. Be particularly careful of drinking on an empty stomach — food helps to mitigate the less pleasant effects of alcohol.
3 If you're going to a party, consider the possibility of having a glass of milk beforehand — this lines and protects the stomach.
4 If you find that you've had more to drink than you intended, then once again have a glass or two of milk — this can have some protective effect on the tum even at this late hour.

'It started out as a hangover, Doctor, but now he seems totally suspended.'

5   If a good deal of wine is being pressed on you, consider the virtues of drinking a little water between whiles, in order to dilute the effect of the alcohol.

6   Most important this — *be wary of drinks that are rich in congeners*. Congener-rich tipples include whisky (and whiskey), brandy, sherry, port, vermouths, and most red wines — (especially the 'rich' and 'heavy' ones, like Chianti.)

You are likely to get particularly vindictive congeners from cheap and nasty red plonks — especially if you are misguided enough to drink the dregs of the bottle. Drinks which are relatively *free* of congeners (and are therefore less likely to induce the dreaded hangover) include champagne, most decent white wines and — surprisingly enough — vodka and gin. But beware of the sheer *power* of spirits — especially late at night. Whisky, gin and vodka are roughly ten times the alcoholic strength of beer — and an extra double late at night may mean a miserable morning.

TREATMENT OF HANGOVERS

I discovered the ultimate 'cure' for the hangover when I attended my fifth Melbourne Cup. The Melbourne Cup is like a glorious Australian mixture of Mardi Gras, Christmas and a Bar Mitzva and the amount of alcohol there is to drink is quite staggering: they start dispensing the champagne at nine in the morning so that by the time you fall into bed you have had a memorable day — even if you don't remember much about it! Well, at last year's Melbourne Cup I met Bob Sangster and he introduced me to some miraculous tablets called Beroccas. They are produced by Roche in Switzerland and distributed under concession to an Australian company. On the label it says they are 'for use in deficiencies caused by infections, pregnancy, alcoholism or liver damage', which means that they solve all of life's problems in one. Don't ask me how Beroccas work, but I promise you they do.

I don't know where outside of Australia one can obtain Beroccas and I do know that doctors maintain there is no real *cure* for the hangover, so the only practical help I can offer you are these few pointers which may help you to make the best of things the morning after the night before.

* *Don't* have a hair of the dog that bit you — this is a good way to start on the road to cirrhosis.
* Instead, drink plenty of fluid. Your body is badly dehydrated — which means that its cells are literally crying out for water.
* If you don't like water, drinks lots of fruit juice. This contains all sorts of goodies (like potassium) and so is actually more reviving that water itself.
* Milk is good too — because it soothes the battered tum.
* Have some food as soon as you can. You may not feel like it, but just as in the case of sea-sickness, it'll do you good: it provides much needed nutriment, and helps to protect your liver.
* *What* you eat doesn't actually matter very much, as long as you eat something. But avoid spicy things — simple food, like soup, cheese sandwiches, and fruit are good.
* Coffee gives you a bit of a lift — but don't drink too much, because it can irritate those already jangling nerve-endings. Tea is O.K.
* If you feel terrible, go to bed and SLEEP.
* Don't drive if you can possibly avoid it. Not only will your driving skills be below par, but there is just a possibility that some alcohol left over from the night before might get you in trouble with the law.

Finally, here are a few traditional hangover remedies. I can't *promise* that they'll help, but they will while away the time till you sober up — or find an Australian chemist to sell you some Beroccas.

Corpse Reviver

1 measure brandy
100 ml (4 oz) milk

1 dash angostura
1 teaspoon sugar

Shake, strain into a tall glass and add soda water.

'*A marvellous cure for hangover, sir. It's 100 % proof.*'

Prairie Oyster

Small wine glass
1 teaspoon Worcester sauce 2 dashes vinegar
1 teaspoon tomato sauce 1 dash pepper
1 unbroken raw yolk of egg
(Close your eyes and down in one!)

Bullshot

Medium sized glass
1 measure vodka 1 dash lemon juice
2 measures condensed 1 dash: Worcester sauce,
  consommé tabasco, cayenne pepper,
2 measures tomato juice and celery salt
Shake.

Bloody Mary

Ferdinand L. Petiot, the barman at Harry's New York bar in Paris, first mixed vodka and tomato juice in 1920. American entertainer Roy Barton called the mixture 'Bucket of Blood' after a club in Chicago. The drink was later named 'The Red Snapper' after Petiot had spiced it up with salt, pepper, lemon and Worcester sauce.

Medium sized glass 2 dashes Worcester sauce
add ice a little lemon juice
1 measure vodka top up with tomato juice
Stir or shake; add extra seasoning, salt, pepper or tabasco if desired.

Snails à la Poulette

First catch your snails (this may be difficult if you have a hangover). Boil them for five minutes, not forgetting to add a pinch of salt. Then shell them and wash them carefully. Drain them, and then simmer for 1½ hours with salt, bay leaves and some parsley.

Meanwhile, back on the range, brown some diced onions, and then add a little of whatever wine you were drinking the night before to the pan, plus a few tablespoonfuls of water. Bring the pan to the boil and then drop in the simmered snails, having first drained them. Let the whole thing boil for five minutes, then squeeze the juice of half a lemon over the top.

Serve. Eat.

If you like snails, you will find this delicious. If you don't, then at least the experience will remind you of the folly of excessive drinking.

THE BODY BEAUTIFUL

The slim-line drinker doesn't have too many hangovers, simply because he doesn't drink too much. Too much booze will make you fat because *all alcohol is packed full of calories*. This is because alcohol itself is a fuel which the body can burn, in the same way that it burns food. If you find this hard to believe, reflect on what happens when you pour a little brandy over your Christmas pudding and light it. The stuff burns — giving out both heat and light. Just that same energy is released in your body, in the form of calories, when you imbibe.

That is why it is almost impossible to slim while regularly taking any significant amount of alcohol. Or, to be more accurate, a moderate but regular drinker could only slim by cutting down on his food intake to such an extent that he'd be jeopardizing his health. (This, unfortunately, is what happens to many alcoholics.) So, if you're overweight and want to slim, your first move must be to cut out alcohol — or at least cut it down to a very low level.

But what about the person who is *not* particularly overweight but who just wants to be able to drink and stay slim? This is not an unreasonable objective, provided that you remember the relatively high calorie content of booze. And — most especially — bear in mind that the stronger the drink, then the more calories it will contain. Spirits — such as whisky, gin, vodka and rum — contain roughly ten times as much alcohol as beer or cider, drop for drop, and

this means ten times as many calories. Most wines contain approximately three times as much alcohol as beer does, and fortified wines (such as port and sherry) and vermouths contain even more — which is why they are so fattening.

Of course, it all depends on how much of each drink you take. Though whisky is about ten times as strong as beer, the man who drinks six pints of bitter a night will quite probably get fat, while the man who drinks two single Scotches probably won't.

There are two other factors which the drinker must keep in mind if he wants to remain slim. The first is the amount of *sweetness* of the drink itself. In other words, some drinks contain sugar as well as alcohol. Clearly, this sugar is itself fattening. So if you have a tendency to develop a touch of *embonpoint*, steer clear of such things as sweet cider, sweet wine, sweet sherry, and sweet liqueurs. Avoid stouts too — a pint of stout contains roughly as many calories as a pint of milk (which is about a tenth of an average man's calorie requirements for the whole day).

Ordinary beers and lagers also contain some fattening carbohydrates in addition to their alcohol content. But it's well worth trying the excellent Pils Lager, which is so low in carbohydrates that it's widely drunk by diabetics. (However, it does contain a lot of alcohol.)

Secondly, there is the question of the *mixers* you use with your drinks. Many of these are sweet — and therefore fattening. Low-calorie mixers, like 'slim-line' bitter lemon are therefore to be applauded.

ALCOHOLIC CALORIE CHART

Here is a brief guide to the calorie content of various drinks. The weight-conscious drinker may care to commit it to mind, or to keep a copy in the drinks cupboard.
Note: The average adult in the developed countries takes

in about 2500 calories a day. A typical slimming diet would contain only 1000 calories a day.

Drink	Calories (approx)
Red wine − small glass	75
Dry white wine − small glass	75
Sweet white wine − small glass	85 or more
Dry sherry − small glass	80
Sweet sherry − small glass	90 or more
Stout one pint	250
Beer or lager − one pint	160
Whisky − one tot	70
Gin − one tot	70
Dry cider − one pint	200
Sweet cider − one pint	250
Vintage cider − one pint	560
Sweet liqueurs − one measure	90 or more

There is no doubt that *excessive* amounts of alcohol do have a rather disastrous effect on a person's appearance over a period of time. You only have to look at certain well-known film stars to see that. Do be wary if you find that after some years of cheerful social drinking, your face is beginning to 'thicken' and your jowls are starting to become ponderous. Cut down on the grog. It is not impossible to get rid of that dreadful flabby boozer's countenance − if you get a move on.

A slight red nose from drinking alcohol is also not irreversible − provided that you keep your drinking within reasonable limits. But if the redness gets worse − to the stage where people start saying, 'Hello, Rudolph' − then it's probably time to give up drinking altogether, unless you wish to be saddled with a real old-fashioned 'grog-blossom' hooter. Plastic surgery will *not* cure this. Similarly with broken veins on the face − these are an indication of trouble. (If the alcohol is doing that to your face, what is it doing to your liver?) Unless you want to be like Bardolph in *Henry IV* Part I, whose booze-soaked countenance was covered in 'meteors' and 'exhalations', you'd better give up the bottle. That said, never forget that moderate drinking is *good for you*! Remember St Paul's advice in his First Epistle to Timothy: 'Use a little wine for thy stomach's sake and thine often infirmities.'

What's more, scientific evidence that wine has 'superior health values' was presented to an international conference at Avignon not long ago by a professor from the University of California. Among the reasons he gave were that: a half-litre of wine provides about 40 % of the average adult's daily iron requirements; wine can be a replacement for carbohydrates, supplying a substantial amount of the body's energy needs; and it contains significant amounts of at least ten vitamins – particularly the B-vitamins like Riboflavin – as well as more than half the twenty 'growth factors' necessary to human well-being.

CHEERS!

Postscript

If you want to have a hangover but you can't afford to drink, these are the pages for you. The jokes are so dreadful they're bound to give you a headache. The inebriated friends who passed them on to me ask to remain anonymous. I'm not at all surprised.

The dancing duck

One spring morning a man walked into a public house on the outskirts of Nottingham just after opening time. Under his arm he carried a biscuit tin with a live duck on top of it performing a rather neat tap dance. He placed the tin with its feathered burden on the bar counter and as the landlord emerged from the rear of the premises called for a pint of bitter. Whilst fulfilling the order the landlord's gaze was riveted on the duck which, by now, was demonstrating an extremely graceful soft shoe shuffle. As he put the pint on the counter the following conversation took place.

'Is that duck yours?'
'Yes.'
'Do you want to sell it?'
'Why?'
'Well, it would make a good draw for my business.'
'How much?'
'Fifty quid.'

'Done.'

As the stranger left, the landlord called after him, 'How do I get him to stop at closing time?'

'Oh, that's easy, just take the lid off the biscuit tin and blow out the candle!'

Water has killed more people than booze.
Remember the Flood?

Drinking doesn't drown your troubles, it just irrigates them.

Two Irishmen were returning home after closing time.
Paddy: 'I got a Guinness for the wife.'
Mick: 'That's a good swap.'

Boss to secretary: 'How about a whisky and sofa?'
Secretary to boss: 'No thanks, just a gin and platonic.'

Paddy went into the bar and ordered nineteen pints because the sign read, NO ONE SERVED UNDER EIGHTEEN.

As the dying midget said; 'I'll have a small bier.'

Dog Nose Rose: Tiger Bay, circa 1958

Dog Nose Rose, so called after her favourite tipple, a mixture of beer and gin. She had everything a man could ask for, big muscles and a hairy chest. . . . In the right light she looked like a million dollars, wrinkled and green. Despite this she did have a heart of gold, yellow and hard.

Drunken beggar: 'Excuse me guv, could you spare a fiver for a pint?'
Man: 'A fiver! but a pint only costs 40p.'
Drunk: 'I know, but I'm a big tipper.'